Computer Monographs

GENERAL EDITOR: Stanley Gill, M.A., Ph.D.
ASSOCIATE EDITOR: J. J. Florentin, Ph.D., Birkbeck College, London

Program Debugging

A

Program Debugging

The Prevention and Cure
of Program Errors

A. R. Brown, M.B.C.S.
OCC Systems Limited

and

W. A. Sampson B.Sc.
Gemini Computer Systems Limited

Macdonald · London and
American Elsevier · New York

© A. R. Brown and W. A. Sampson, 1973

Sole distributors for the British Isles and Commonwealth
Macdonald & Co. (Publishers) Ltd.
49–50 Poland Street, London W.1

Sole distributors for the United States and Dependencies
American Elsevier Publishing Company Inc.
52 Vanderbilt Avenue, New York, N.Y. 10017

All remaining areas
Elsevier Publishing Company
P.O. Box 211, Jan van Galenstraat 335, Amsterdam, The Netherlands

Macdonald ISBN 0 356 04267 7
American Elsevier ISBN 0 444 19565 3
Library of Congress Catalog Card No 72-12417

Made and printed in Great Britain by
Balding + Mansell Ltd, London and Wisbech

Contents

Part III—Bug identification and elimination

Preface

The essential material of this book was researched for a course on Debugging Techniques, which has been successfully presented on a number of occasions. When we started work on that material the common reaction of people we spoke to was one of amazement: debugging is considered a kind of formless, esoteric art, only learnt by programmers through trial and error and almost impossible to discover techniques for it, let alone teach them.

Our aim is to take the mystique out of debugging. It is a technique that *can* be formulated, although few people have tried to do so comprehensively in the past. After a literature search we have only been able to find a smallish number of (in the main) highly specific papers. Most programming courses tend to mention briefly the diagnostic facilities of the language concerned but do not cover the general techniques of testing at all.

The majority of commercial programmers spend as much as 50% of their time program testing but all their formal training and development is concentrated in the other half of their jobs. There is an enormous pool of inefficiency and inaccuracy waiting to be drained: millions of pounds a year are spent worldwide on debugging and even a small increase in efficiency will save a great deal of money. It is our view that the standard of testing in every installation could be improved to some degree.

The purpose of this book is to give ideas on how bugs can be prevented in the first place and, once they are in, as they inevitably will be, how they can be found and removed as quickly as possible.

Acknowledgements

The authors would like to thank Gemini Computer Systems Limited —for whom the basic material was developed—for permission to write this book. We must acknowledge the contribution of the many Gemini staff members who also worked on the project. Thanks are also due to Wendy Daybell, Maureen Sampson and Janet Knaggs for their sterling secretarial assistance.

Part I Introductory

1 Introduction

1.1 Setting the context

1.1.1 Historical development

Today's computer society is now in the latest of three discernible phases in its development:

First of all, computers were toys for mathematicians and electronics engineers. Few other people came into contact with them and they had little direct impact on society. It was during this period that the super-technical, 'boffin' image grew around the early machines.

Then came the long period of expansion and glamour which only ended around the beginning of 1971. All sorts of exaggerated claims were made for the benefits that these machines would bring to society and there were positive fears by some that computers would 'take over the world'. Generally computing was oversold—the panacea for all management and administrative ills.

Finally we have the present situation: there is fairly wide exposure of the general public to the use of computers, or, rather, to some of the more pedestrian and bug-ridden systems developed in the fields of invoicing, public utility billing, etc. More or less the only publicity DP systems receive is the popular anti-computer story. Our present social climate emphasises the importance of individual privacy and there are very active lobbies devoted to minimising the creation of databanks of personal information. Some even go so far as to list computers amongst napalm, nuclear weapons, etc., as the cancerous evils of our present society.

In the commercial context, companies are growing to be more concerned with testing expensive service operations—such as a computer installation—against the yardstick of cost-effectiveness, rather than with justifying their existence on the grounds of prestige, etc., which has been common earlier.

1

Computer installations used to be regarded, indulgently, as show-places by their owners and as proof of our developing technology by society at large. In that situation there was no real incentive to penalise sloppy work. Now the spotlight is on: installations must improve their organisation, methods, standards and competence if they are to play their true economic and social role.

We see this book as a contribution to help DP become more cost-effective.

1.1.2 Why computer systems do not work

Whoever you speak to, it is always someone else's fault: operators blame programmers, programmers blame systems analysts, analysts blame users and users blame all of the others! Assuming the data input is correct, there are five possible types of error 'internal' to a DP system: hardware, software, operating, programming, and systems. We shall be discussing them all to a certain extent in this book, but will concentrate on systems and programming errors as they are the most common. Perhaps most of all we shall be concentrating on the mystique-ridden program error.

Our own estimates of the relative incidence of types of error dictate our approach, and are shown in the following table. We would point out most strongly that the estimates are intuitive, very rough and refer to the average commercial installation.

Percentage of system failures due to	
Hardware	1%
Software	2%
Operating	5%
Programming	90%
Systems	2%

1.1.3 Consequences of program errors

As program (or programmer) errors are the most numerous, it is worth looking at the major consequences of them.

Firstly there are the costs of testing and correcting programs. As much as 50% of the average commercial programmer's time is spent on debugging, and during this time he is making heavy use of the machine. It has been suggested that the manpower costs alone could be as much as £40m per year in the U.K., plus machine time and concealed costs such as re-runs of live systems and misuse of the best-qualified personnel who are called in to assist in the 'baling out' situations.

Secondly there is the frustration of the programmer's creative talents: many programmers feel their work is done when the program is coded, and they are anxious to get on to crack the next new problem. Debugging usually takes place in an atmosphere of impatience. In fact the origin of the word 'bug' to mean program(mer) error is an effort by programmers to preserve their sanity: that many errors would not be psychologically acceptable, so malicious beasts that have infested the program are blamed!

Lastly there is the effect of errors on users and victims. An incorrect program is worth less than no program at all because of the false conclusions it may inspire. There is always someone ready to seize on mistakes and blame the computer, or the people who run it. As automated control systems become more common—control of a moonshot, medical systems, etc.—a program error could really cause deaths.

1.2 Types of error

1.2.1 Inter-relation of errors

Let us take a closer look at the nature of errors and their inter-connection. Hardware errors are mercifully rare nowadays and are often easily detected: the program produces obviously wrong results or simply will not run at all. An intermittent hardware error can be extremely difficult to detect, however, and may persist for a long time before it can be pinned down.

Software errors are also generally fairly rare (although some systems and installations are plagued with them), but they are almost always extremely difficult to detect. We shall be talking about them at length later. Usually the program is blamed first and software (or hardware) only as a last resort, so these types are inherently costly and time-wasting.

Systems, programming and operating errors are often difficult to distinguish and often inter-related. For example, bad systems design can lead to undue operating difficulties and ambiguity to bad program specification, so that programs can be correctly written to solve the wrong problems.

1.2.2 Program errors

By far the most numerous and complicated are program errors. They can be divided into three categories:

1. Appreciation errors—failure to read a specification thoroughly before starting work.

2. Logic errors imply failure to 'think through' the problem at a detailed level.

3. Coding errors, which can be further subdivided into:

(a) Syntax errors—improper use of the language statements. These are often detected and rejected by the compiler.

(b) Structural errors are concerned with the interaction of statements or blocks of statements and may or may not be detected by the compiler.

(c) Transcription errors are handwriting slips. Some will be detected by a compiler but many will not, the syntax and structure being perfectly legal.

1.3 Purpose of this book

We shall be dealing with work methods and specific techniques that minimise the incidence of all types of error mentioned above. Mainly the emphasis will be on program errors, as extensive forays into systems analysis or operating would be inappropriate.

For management, we aim to set out work methods and an approach to programming which minimise the probability of program errors. We shall analyse the influence of various technical factors on errors and describe and evaluate specific debugging techniques.

Senior programmers should be able to use the book as a basis upon which to redesign programming standards.

Programmers should be able to modify their approach to the design and writing of programs in such a way as to become significantly more productive in the future.

The approach is deliberately highly practical: an actual, realistic program is included to illustrate the use of the recommended design standards and each step in the writing and testing of the program is described in detail to illustrate the working of the recommended methods.

2 Language considerations

The particular language used in writing a program clearly has an impact on the ease of debugging that program, but it is only rarely possible for a programmer to choose his language in order to minimise his debugging problems. Well-run installations will have standardised on the language to be used and the circumstances under which a particular language must be used. The choice will have been influenced by ease of debugging, certainly, but efficiency, ease of program amendment, facilities supported by the language, and so on, will probably have been factors at least as important in the choice. Thus the programmer with a given program to write will almost certainly have no individual choice of language open to him.

However, the programmer can make the best of what he may consider to be a bad job by knowing in which respects the particular language he is using affects debugging, be it either favourably or unfavourably, but we will concentrate mainly on the question of the level of language used and its influence upon certain aspects of program debugging.

2.1 Levels of language

Four language levels are commonly recognised, although others do exist: these four are machine code, low level (often called assembler or autocode), high level (e.g. the industry-wide languages like Cobol and Fortran), and ultra high level (e.g. Cobol program generators).

It is extremely unusual to find machine code used in a normal installation, its use now being largely confined to software writing, although even here it is not uncommon to find high level languages being used. For example Algol compilers are often written in Algol itself.

On the other hand, many installations will use both low and high level languages together, usually the machine's assembler and Cobol, but there are still many users who use assembler language only, although the reverse—using Cobol only—is relatively rare.

The ultrahigh level language is almost exclusively used as an adjunct to the main language of an installation, but there are some users who depend entirely upon such languages. The languages generally offer either very quick and easy programming or a specialised ability, or both (for example, file management or information retrieval), but are usually relatively inefficient in terms of machine usage. However, programs generated in this way are often only run once, or are run on a very *ad hoc* basis, so that the expenditure of a great deal of programming effort to improve efficiency is simply not justified.

2.2 Debugging problems and language levels

2.2.1 Syntax errors

Because lower level languages use simpler and less powerful statements than higher level languages, it follows that the syntax of those statements must be simpler and so less prone to error. For instance, a multiply statement in an assembler language will usually put the answer in a pre-determined location, whereas the Cobol statement MULTIPLY STONES BY 14 implies that the result is to be stored in the literal, which is incorrect syntax: either a GIVING clause has been omitted or else the order of the operands is wrong. Although the compiler will usually find errors of this kind, it is advisable to check the logic of the statement, too, because although MULTIPLY A BY B is valid from a syntax viewpoint, it is logically incorrect if the result is required in A rather than in B.

2.2.2 Logic errors

There should be no difference on this score between language levels, but we have just seen a case in which a high level language could produce a logic error where the low level one could not, and it is in this area of the misuse of the power of higher level languages that logic errors can arise. Compound or nested IF statements, for instance, are favourite vehicles for displaying the expertise of some

7

programmers. But they are extremely difficult to get right, even in simple cases, mainly because all the true/false combinations are just not considered. Even in a very simple compound condition such as

```
IF A OR B
THEN statement-1
ELSE statement-2
```

it is often only the paths for both-true and both-false that are checked out during coding. The one-true/one-false situations are just not considered, with the obvious result.

2.2.3 'Detail' errors

These are the sort of errors that one makes through sheer careless-ness, and are therefore often errors of omission: omission of punctua-tion, or heading, or directives are common examples. Although the incidence of such errors may be roughly equal for each level of language, the higher the level the more likely it is that the compiler can make an intelligent guess, substitute what it thinks should have been there, and can then carry on, so that the effect of these errors is less. In addition, of course, the use of libraries of data descriptions, particularly in Cobol, reduces quite dramatically the incidence of this sort of error.

2.2.4 Compiler errors

The higher the level of language, the more complicated the compiler, and so the more errors it is likely to contain. As is explained in Chapter 14, these errors can often be difficult to find and to prove, and may be quite awkward to bypass. The topic is mentioned again below.

2.2.5 Diagnostics

There is little doubt that high level language compilers produce more and better diagnostics than low level language ones, but this ad-vantage is often marred by the production of many consequential errors from a single actual error. Apart from being distinctly em-barrassing, this propensity can cause some real errors to be missed, and can therefore waste a compilation.

2.2.6 Use of language

This is more a question of efficiency than of debugging, but it is worth saying that an assembler programmer, used to doing everything for himself, through procedures, will often not appreciate what is perhaps the most fundamental point in the efficient use of a high level language: that thoughtful data description can eliminate the need for whole sections of procedure. Similarly, unintelligent use of the language by programmers unfamiliar with the computer's architecture can result in gross inefficiencies, for instance doing arithmetic on the ICL 1900 on DISPLAY fields instead of on fields described as COMPUTATIONAL SYNCHRONISED RIGHT. The solution to both of these points lies in education: in the philosophy of the language, on the one hand, and of the machine, on the other.

2.3 Choice of compiler

For programmers in most situations the question of which compiler to use is as academic as that of which language to use, because with a given language in a given installation he may have no choice at all. The installation will almost certainly have settled on a compiler level that suits its configuration and/or ambitions. Other compilers may just not run on the configuration concerned, or the installation may simply not have updated the other compilers, possibly in order to avoid their use. However, a particular program may require language facilities that are only supported by a higher level compiler, and in such cases the installation may allow the use of the 'non-standard' compiler, either on their own machine or else through a time-sharing or conventional bureau.

2.3.1 What makes a good compiler

One might define the ideal compiler as one that has good diagnostics, is free of errors, will generate efficient coding, gives good documentation, and compiles quickly. Obviously some of these—for example speed and efficiency—cannot exist together in full measure, and one

9

does not always want the full amount of documentation, so it is very convenient to have the ability to choose which facilities one uses. It is particularly useful to be able to have a 'testing' and a 'production' type of compilation, either through options within the compiler, or through two separate compilers. This would mean that a compilation during testing would be quick, rather than efficient, and would miss out any optional documentation, whereas the compilation to produce an operational program would be efficient and would give full documentation. A final test must always be carried out in these circumstances on the optimised version in case any errors have been introduced by the optimisation.

2.3.2 Compatibility

Programs written in one of the industry-compatible languages (with the possible exception of Fortran) have not in the past been as portable as one would like. Yet one of the main reasons for using such languages is to make one's programs independent of one's hardware, thereby giving freedom of choice when changing computers by minimising or eliminating the reprogramming problems. Apart from problems caused by differences in machine architecture, programs are often not portable because facilities supported by one manufacturer's compiler are not supported by the other manufacturer. This sort of situation can arise because one manufacturer may offer more power, by means of SORT or COMPUTE verbs, for instance, or may offer the ability to use machine features like sense switches. There are relatively few installations or programmers who can resist the temptation to use such appealing features; it seems such a shame to waste them. But it is clear that the temptation should be resisted, and it would be nice if it did not exist.

In Cobol, at least, the situation has been improved by the insistence of the U.S. Department of Defense that all computers purchased by the Department should have an ANSI Cobol compiler, and the U.S. Navy vetting routines enable compilers and programs to be checked for conformity with the standard. So our advice is, if an ANSI Cobol compiler is provided with your computer, use it; and if one is not, try to use only those facilities that would be included in an ANSI compiler if you had one.

3 Debugging aids

For the purpose of this book we will define a debugging aid as any automatic aid that helps produce correct programs faster, and it is therefore apparent from this definition that there are many aids that we could consider, ranging from print utilities to modular testbeds to program generators. We will restrict our main discussion to the types of aid that are widely used, in order not to spend too much time on testing aids to which most programmers do not have access. In doing this we are by no means suggesting that the less common aids are not useful, simply that in a book of this nature we must consciously direct our remarks to the majority, in order that our message gets across clearly. We will briefly mention other aids to complete the spectrum.

This chapter divides debugging aids into different classes and describes each class separately, the aim being to encourage the reader to consider whether he should be using a particular class of aid, and also to consider whether he could find a better aid of a class that he is already using, perhaps with disappointing results so far.

3.1 Debugging aids and language level

At one time certain whole classes of aid were only applicable to a particular level of language. This has now changed and pretty well all classes of aid are now available with each of the two main language levels.

3.2 Popular debugging aids and their use

3.2.1 Classification

Popular debugging aids may be classified as follows:

    (a) Test data dispersion utilities
    (b) Print utilities

(c) Module testing packages
(d) In-built language facilities
(e) Programmed-in aids
(f) Post-mortem dumps
(g) Source code amendment facilities

Some of these are obviously more intimately concerned with the program under test that others, and it is in these classes that some dependence upon the actual language used does still exist.

3.2.2 Test data dispersion utilities

These are used to create a file of test data on (usually) magnetic tape or disc from a punched card or paper tape file of test data. If one is available—and they are by no means universally so—then the expense and drudgery of writing and testing a special program to create the file is completely eliminated.

Although these programs create files, they do not create *data*, merely dispersing the input test data on to the output test file. Even so they are extremely important and useful, and every installation without one, or without a good one, should certainly think about acquiring or writing one.

A good utility of this type will have a number of characteristics: it will allow field conversion—for instance, a decimal number input could be converted to binary or packed decimal format on the output file; it will allow blank fields to be omitted, so that a programmer setting up a large record, of which his program uses only a few fields, would be able to specify only those fields in which he is interested; it will allow long records to be set up from a series of punched cards or paper tape input.

A bad one, on the other hand, will almost certainly require the card or paper tape input record to contain a picture—sometimes in hexadecimal or octal—of the input record to be created, and in these cases the utility is little more than a straight card to magnetic tape or disc transcription program.

3.2.3 File print utilities

This class of aid is used to print back files created by the program under test, usually from magnetic tape or disc. Such programs are available and used universally, and are usually quite adequate, although some are better than others. For instance, the better ones will: start each new record on a new line; print several representations of each word, for example hexadecimal or octal, character, and signed decimal; stop at the end of the file. Even so, problems can still arise if one wishes to print the contents of a non-standard file, or if the file contains multi-word values, binary fractions or floating-point numbers.

3.2.4 Module testing packages

Packages such as this greatly assist in the testing of separately developed modules of a program, because they provide a test 'harness' into which individual modules can be 'plugged' for testing. More will be said about these aids and their uses in Part IV.

3.2.5 In-built language facilities and programmed-in aids

These two classes of aid are very similar in use, both actually being used within (or effectively within) the program during the course of a test, a separate monitoring program sometimes being used to give this effect. The distinction between them is real but perhaps rather academic: in-built language facilities are statements that form part of the language specification and that are specifically meant for program debugging, while programmed-in aids are normal language facilities that are used in a somewhat artificial fashion in order to produce debugging information. The effect is largely the same, but in-built debugging facilities are easier to use.

The best example of a language with in-built aids is PL/1, which has superb facilities for debugging including an excellent snapshot and trace, and a range of ON conditions to detect errors such as conversion errors, subscript range errors, and so on, that would normally cause program failure.

To get any significant debugging assistance in most implementations of Cobol, on the other hand, one has to program-in the aids, generally using the DISPLAY verb to print or punch monitoring information, although trace facilities are sometimes provided.

The interesting thing about these aids is not their difference, but their similarity in the sense that they provide the programmer with tools that he can use to monitor the operation of his program during a test shot. Unfortunately, as far as most programmers are concerned, the tools are not really necessary, being used (if at all) only when all else fails to solve a particular problem.

We believe so strongly that use of this sort of aid provides the best, easiest, fastest, and most certain way to a properly and fully tested program that much of Chapter 6 has been devoted to their use.

3.2.6 Post-mortem dumps

In a welfare state the sordid and debasing business of searching rubbish dumps for food and clothing is usually rendered unnecessary by the provision of the various welfare benefits, although there are rare cases where such benefits are not obtainable, so one may have to resort to dump-combing. Similarly, we believe that programmers who earn their living by scratching about in program dumps are engaging in a rather sordid and inefficient practice that can usually be wholly avoided by planning and executing program testing in the more efficient ways that we describe later.

Dumps do have some uses, and the IBM 360/370 dump is planned as a debugging aid and so is rather more helpful than most, but essentially the use of dumps, particularly when debugging high level language programs, is not, we believe, good programming practice.

3.2.7 Source code amendment facilities

These facilities can range from simple card or paper tape amendment programs to powerful source program library and maintenance systems, such as ICL 1900 COSY (COmpilation SYstem). In either case they avoid the errors inherent in manual updating of a source deck, but machine access is required to use the facility, and in using even the simple ones, mistakes can be made.

In the majority of cases the most satisfactory solution is to maintain the source on magnetic tape or disc and to amend it through such a facility, which may in fact be provided by the compiler itself, as in ICL 1900 Cobol, for instance.

14

3.3 More exotic aids

This section covers the more unusual aids like test data generators, pre-processors, flowcharters and cross-reference listers, all of which can provide quite sophisticated assistance.

3.3.1 Test data generators

We mentioned earlier that test data dispersion utilities do not create data, but there are programs that do. Such facilities are usually part of a larger package and they will generate numeric fields, alphabetic fields, bad data, related fields, fields within limits, and so on. It is particularly useful when such packages can utilise existing data descriptions in the program for record layouts and file attributes and devices.

3.3.2 Pre-processors

A wide variety of facilities is available under this general heading. For instance:
  (a) Syntax checking.
  (b) 'Shorthand' expansion/conversion: this covers the conversion of 'shorthand' pre-source code into actual source code. Into this category fall decision table pre-processors (as opposed to direct decision table compilers, which are really a kind of high level language).
  (c) Formatted listing.
  (d) Warnings on bad programming practices and improper use of language.

3.3.3 Automatic flowcharters

Originally, these were used on a bureau basis to flowchart a program that was about to be amended and whose documentation was suspect, but nowadays many installations are using them on their own machines to provide the flowcharts in the first place, thus removing an unpopular chore, giving absolute conformity to flowcharting standards, and simplifying the amendment of program flowcharts when the program is altered. Machine-drawn flowcharts are an acquired taste, and are really not ideal, but at least they are standard and predictable, and they probably represent the only realistic route to provide up-to-date, detailed program flowcharts. An example of part of such a flowchart is given for our case study program in Appendix 4.

3.3.4 Cross-reference listers

Cross-reference listings are very useful when amending programs, and are provided by some compilers, notably by ANSI Cobol ones. Even if one's compiler cannot produce such a listing, a suitable package can usually be bought or written quite cheaply.

Part II Bug avoidance

4 Staff considerations

The basic philosophy of this book centres around the old adage that prevention is better than cure. Propounding techniques that will help you find program errors more efficiently is not enough in itself; we must talk about ways of avoiding them altogether.

There is often a tendency amongst programmers to measure their prowess by the speed with which they can get a program 'on the machine' after receiving some sort of specification. True enough, speed is important but it is speed in producing a working program, not speed in getting it 'on the machine', that matters.

Not all causes of program errors are within the control of the programmer. There are much wider issues—such as the quality, housing and organisation of staff and the work standards they are expected to follow—that have just as much effect on the incidence of bugs as the programming techniques adopted by the individual. In this chapter and those immediately following we will examine some of these broad subjects which nevertheless affect the way a programmer works.

4.1 Organisation structure

4.1.1 Relevance to debugging

A DP department that is well structured allows a two-way flow of confidence. On one side the management are able to exercise close supervision and can therefore have confidence in the way the work is progressing. From the other side, a programmer needs to have confidence in the people who are supervising his work, as does everyone of course, but this is particularly important for anyone doing a job with a creative element. An orderly department leads to orderly programming.

4.1.2 Communication between analyst and programmer

Obviously good, clear communication of ideas is essential. If the programmer does not clearly know what he is trying to achieve he is hardly likely to produce useful results. Ideally the senior programmer should be involved in the later stages of systems design, but the basic medium of communication must be the written one. The need for good standards of presentation is clear. It is important that any systems errors be eliminated before programming commences or they can cause havoc when discovered later. The involvement of a number of people—including a senior programmer—in the detailed design work should help to find these errors of systems logic.

4.1.3 Communication between programmer and operator

It is imperative that the operator knows exactly how the program is to be run: what peripherals are in use, and unusual happenings, what to do if it fails, how it can fail, how to stop it if necessary, what run time is expected, etc. Again it is a question of standards for presentation of all appropriate information to the operators.

Besides this, a good working relationship between the programming and operations units is essential. Internecine warfare in the department (not at all uncommon in our experience) can cause nothing but problems for the installation as a whole.

4.1.4 Type of structures

In practice, no two computer departments seem to have exactly the same organisational structures, but broad patterns are discernible. The most common organisation is to separate the programming and systems functions into separate units, under a Chief Programmer and a Chief Systems Analyst, these two plus the Operations Manager reporting direct to the departmental manager. Some installations favour the 'analyst/programmer' concept. Systems work and programming are done by the same group of people who form a kind of spectrum: a junior person will be 100% occupied with programming and a very senior one almost entirely with higher-level systems work, but the bulk of people in between are concerned with a degree of systems work (appropriate to their development) *and* programming.

18

In this situation there tends to be just one person in charge of the hybrid team, usually called Systems & Programming Manager.

Besides Systems, Programming and Operations (which includes data preparation personnel), some DP departments have within them an O & M unit. In other companies O & M (if it exists as a specific skill) is organised as a unit on a par with DP within a composite Management Services Department. The permutations of these basic options seem endless in practice.

4.1.5   Which is best?

It is our view that separation of systems and programming functions is 'best' *from the work-accuracy viewpoint.* Obviously communication problems arise with this that just do not exist if the same man is both specifying and writing a program. But separation should mean better documentation and better error-spotting—the programmer having to work out the program requirements from written specifications will soon complain if they are inadequate, and is more likely to find errors in the design than the analyst working from his own rough notes. There is a strong argument too for having a clean break between design work and programming: with an analyst/programmer at work the processes tend to be merged and are therefore more difficult for the supervisor to control.

'Best' from the accuracy point of view is not necessarily best for the company. The pros and cons of the alternative structures can be (and frequently are) argued interminably but there is no organisation clearly superior on all counts to the others, hence the diversity of structures found in use. All sorts of factors (such as overall management structure, size of department, company-wide grading structures, the need to build from an existing nucleus and, of course, the preferences of the DP Manager) must be taken into account. We say that the increased accuracy resulting from separated systems and programming functions is one important factor that should not be forgotten.

4.1.6   Within the programming function

Whatever the split of systems and programming work, there will almost certainly be further fragmentation of duties within the programming function. To a certain extent these depend on size—a three-man department is hardly likely to have a separate software section—but any department of more than, say, 10 people usually starts to exhibit some programming specialisation. The usual splits are between new development and 'maintenance' work, with 'software' a common third subsection.

Software section

This is a useful section in a large department and is usually responsible for keeping operating systems and program libraries up to date, advising on packages, software development, and so on, and leaves the rest of the programmers free to concentrate on applications programming.

Maintenance section

Generally this is regarded as a necessary evil to cope with the two kinds of maintenance problem: modifications to operational programs and immediate 'repair work' to programs that have broken down in use. The second type of work is usually done under pressure, as a production run is being held up by the fault. Installations therefore tend to use some of their best programmers for urgent repairs, instead of reserving them for new development work only. The larger modification jobs are often treated as new development, so leaving the Maintenance Section only the boring minor modifications to work upon.

Maintenance work has the reputation amongst DP staff—justifiably to a large extent—of being boring, soul-destroying and somehow a second-rate job. It is often difficult to keep maintenance staff busy all the time. The DP Manager must do everything possible to counter these objections or staff will simply evaporate from the Maintenance Section; he might then have to recruit straight into it, further diluting its capabilities. There are a number of actions that can be taken:

    (a) The Maintenance Section should be given as much standing and prestige as possible within the department.

    (b) Staff should be rotated between maintenance and development work—on fixed timetables.

20

(c) The section *should* be given any substantial modification work that comes along, even if it would normally be classed as new development.

All this sounds like a good reason for not having a separate maintenance unit at all and many large installations do indeed get along without the split. Generally speaking, though, there *are* benefits of specialisation and familiarity with existing systems to be gained, despite the organisational problems.

Development section

New projects are developed here, unhindered by problems of software and the necessity of having to go back to old systems. The quality of the work turned out by this section is vitally important as it obviously dictates the amount of running-repair maintenance work in the future. It is in the development teams especially that the messages put over later in this book really need to sink home.

The usual method of organisation within the unit is to have team leaders with nominated team members, working on a specific project or group of connected projects. It is also quite common to have a pool of programmers allocated to teams on a program-by-program basis as needed. There are several variations possible but there is no recognisable 'best' approach: personal qualities of the staff involved are the main consideration, as happy development staff will produce better systems.

Relevance of these splits

Fragmentation of the programming section means that staff can specialise and so improve the speed and standard of the work within their specialisation. Fewer errors should be written into systems and snags discovered should be sorted out more quickly. A multi-unit structure also provides a basis for movement to develop a career.

4.2 The environment

Perfect working conditions will not necessarily mean perfect work but poor conditions will definitely lead to discontent, complaints, lack

21

of enthusiasm and consequently shoddy work.

Generally, very large offices should be avoided for 'creative' personnel such as programmers. Open-plan offices can be noisy and visually distracting and often create an active 'social chat' network. All these things work against concentration and a programmer does need to concentrate for quite long stretches of time. Obviously heating, lighting and ventilation, if inadequate, can ruin concentration too.

It is not essential for efficiency that the office be physically near to the computer room, but what is important is the system of transmitting program tests to and from the machine. Having programmers make long treks several times a day to deliver and pick up test shots is clearly unproductive, and they should either be near to facilities or there should be a good messenger service connecting the two.

All office staff need refreshment facilities but what is often overlooked is that programmers commonly work outside normal office hours: a travelling refreshment trolley mornings and afternoons is no help to a tired programmer at 3 o'clock in the morning. If this is a problem, vending machines for drinks and light snacks should be considered. Such small improvements in the welfare of programmers could lead to better work and therefore fewer errors in programs.

4.3 Quality of staff

Ultimately quality of work depends on quality of staff; but what is 'quality' in relation to DP staff? Does it refer to the whizz-kid genius who gets the job done quickly (perhaps sacrificing standards) or to the slower and steadier worker who gets there in the end, maintaining the standards required throughout? The answer will usually depend upon the installation or the particular situation. We would suggest that the whizz-kid is only really useful in a crisis situation or for one-off jobs or in the software section, because no installation can afford to sacrifice ease of maintenance for speed of development except in an emergency. First class staff are difficult to get *and* difficult to keep.

4.3.1 Recruitment

Great care should be taken in recruiting DP staff. It is easy for bad work not to come to light for months after a poor programmer has been engaged. He may produce his work on time and be outwardly productive but the internal design of the programs might be inefficient and they may be poorly tested, producing a spate of errors when they go operational.

4.3.2 Retaining staff

One of the most desirable qualities of staff is company loyalty but it is not easy to induce this in a breed of people who often think of themselves as DP men first and employees of the company a poor second.

It is clearly necessary to pay 'market rates' to retain good DP staff. An installation that insists on paying the minimum level of salaries it can get away with will, sooner or later, end up with a bevy of people of minimal abilities who simply cannot get better paid jobs because they are not good enough. Money is not the only consideration: some people regard job satisfaction as being marginally more important and they will take less pay in exchange for interesting and rewarding work. It is generally impossible to please everyone all the time and all the manager can do is spread around the interesting and challenging work to try to keep most people happy.

Good career prospects need to be maintained through such devices as training, promoting from within where feasible, movement between sections of the department, and so on. Staff often become dispirited if 'chained' to the same project for a long time and the installation should accept the familiarisation overhead of transferring someone else into a project to relieve a person who wants a change. Generally speaking, DP staff expect to be kept reasonably busy—under-employed staff get lethargic and bored and produce sloppy work.

4.4 Control

It would be impossible—and irrelevant—to deal with the subject of project control at any length here, but a few comments seem in order.

One of the essential features of project control must be the maintenance of laid-down standards (dealt with in detail in the next chapter), but this is often overlooked in the desire to meet target dates.

Work estimates are very dependent on quality of staff and a by-product of the project control system used ought to be person-by-person performance standards that can be used for future estimating. A programmer will not work well unless he feels the targets he is set are achievable. Estimates do tend to be based on either 'We have so much time to do it in' or 'We have so much time, what can we do in that time?'. Both approaches are undesirable, the correct one being: 'That is what we have to do; how long will it take?'.

It is difficult at times to impose a discipline on time-keeping in a programming section due to the abnormal hours often worked. If the staff are responsible enough, a free view should be taken and a minimum of detailed supervision imposed. If they cannot be trusted to those lengths then a compromise system will have to be reached.

When creative work is under way, this should be recognised: when a person is really 'in the mood', he can often work at something all night but, on an 'off day', he may as well pack up and go home. Woolly thinking breeds bugs.

4.5   Don't pamper them

We may have given the impression—discussing the factors that can detract from or upset a programmer's work—that they are a delicate, sensitive race of people, temperamental in the extreme. That was not the intention and programmers certainly should *not* be pampered: that will produce bugs too! It is up to the manager to maintain a good, bug-free standard of work *and* maintain discipline. This chapter has suggested some of the factors that can work against accurate programming and that, generally, should be correctable.

5 Programming standards

In a very real sense this whole book is concerned with programming standards, but not with programming standards as they are generally understood. So, while the rest of it deals with program *debugging* standards, this chapter looks at programming standards as a whole, and aims particularly to mention the relevance of these standards to program debugging.

As we cannot hope to cover the subject to any great depth here, we shall concentrate on the areas in which standards are required and on the reasons for having standards at all. We will not be recommending detailed standards directly, although in the debugging case study we have worked to a reasonably good set of standards that follow the guidelines laid down in this (and other) chapters.

5.1 Purpose of programming standards

Programming standards have two basic purposes, the first of which is to improve programmer performance and the second to improve the management and control of the programming staff.

5.2 Programming standards and programmer performance

5.2.1 Program development

In many ways computer staff, and programmers in particular, still regard themselves as creative artists, and they propound the theory that programming standards restrict their creativity, and so the benefits to be gained from them. But in fact the bulk of the programming done today is relatively straightforward commercial work and, while some parts of this are certainly quite creative and thus highly satisfying to do, the great bulk of the work is, if not simple, at least routine. As such it is very amenable to standardisation and therefore better control.

Standardisation of the programming task, properly done, allows the programmer to give more attention to the interesting parts of his work, because he can simply 'turn the handle' and, without much thought or effort on his behalf, the standard tasks are done— standardly. This process of turning the handle is made easier when the computer itself is made to do some of the mundane jobs: use of standard record and file descriptions through a library, and production of flowcharts automatically are the most obvious examples.

The concentration by the programmer on the parts of his job that he likes best enables him to perform better in those areas, and the removal from him of those parts of his job that he likes least enables him to perform better in those areas also. Thus all round performance improves both in writing the program and in testing it—for the standard parts require no real testing. The result is higher quality programs developed in a shorter time by less frustrated programmers.

5.2.2 Program maintenance

Use of the word frustration reminds us that initial development is only a part, and sometimes only a minor part, of the load upon a programming department. Program maintenance is the other part and, as we said in the last chapter, it is usually the least popular part. The constant use of good programming standards guarantees that the maintenance of programs is made very much easier and more accurate, and for many installations this is therefore the most important aspect of the use of tight programming standards.

5.2.3 Programmer training

Instruction in programming techniques is still relatively rare, and attendance on a language course does not immediately make a trainee an experienced programmer; and, because they have been given no instruction in programming techniques, a dozen different programmers will often approach the same task in a dozen different ways. More alarming, the same programmer is quite capable of doing the same task himself in two or three ways, sometimes unconsciously, but quite often simply for a change, or to provide elegant variation, or to find a way that will take less core or time.

Fierce pride in one's own pet method, or simply difficulties in communicating with each other, tend to retain the *status quo*, and only rigidly enforced programming standards will avoid this type of situation developing. For there is no reason at all why a standard method of carrying out common tasks should not be written down and used, and thus the standards manual takes on the aspect of a training document too. It gives new recruits the distilled results of many years of experience on a plate, and in this way the constant re-invention of the wheel is avoided but, more important, the invention of square wheels is made impossible.

Again, the more automatic one can make the use of these standard routines the better, and the provision of subroutine, macro, or module libraries is thus ideal.

5.3 Programming standards and management control

The use of procedure and performance standards allows any activity to be monitored and controlled, provided only that reporting is done properly. Procedure standards provide a gauge alongside which progress can be measured, because the standards identify a number of break points, the hitting of which is reportable. Performance standards are initially rule of thumb, but are refined as historical data and estimating improve; effectively the performance standards provide the scale to be used on the gauge of the procedure standard.

There is essentially no good reason why sound, well-proven management methods should not be applied to the management of computer programming. That such application is currently the exception rather than the rule proves not that the methods are inapplicable, but that the programming managers are not capable of, or are not interested in, applying them.

Most people in the computer business today recognise that the honeymoon period is over, the recession of 1971 providing ample proof of this. As we pointed out in Chapter 1, the glamour has gone, and with it the endless pouring of money into the unthinking application of computers to the business. From now on, the investment in the Computer Department will be judged according to the same criterion that is applied to any other investment—the return on it.

5.4 The scope of programming standards

5.4.1 Procedure standards

Standards in this area set out to ensure that the programmer goes through the required work stages using the right techniques and there is therefore less chance of skimping. As far as debugging is concerned, the importance lies in the stress upon bug avoidance and thorough testing.

The standards should cover:

(a) Program design, i.e. the modularisation or segmenting of the program. This includes all the rules about the size, shape and number of modules in a program. We examine modular programming in Chapters 6 and 12 and discuss monolithic program design also in Chapter 6.

(b) Flowcharting, which is discussed further in Chapter 7.

(c) Coding, including the use of any standard techniques and the avoidance of any 'dangerous' instructions like ALTER in Cobol. Chapter 7 talks further on this topic.

(d) Desk checking and dry running, which are defined and discussed in Chapter 7.

(e) Testing, including punching and compilation, test data design, logging of test results and the identification and elimination of bugs. The use of debugging aids will also be covered under this heading, although the use of the programmed-in aids should properly be included in the standards for program design.
Chapters 7, 8, 9 and 11 all have a lot more to say on the question of program testing, while the use of debugging aids was covered in Chapter 3.

(f) Program maintenance, which is covered briefly in Chapter 8.

5.4.2 Documentation standards

Ideally, program documentation, being a routine task, should be done by the computer, and the basis of this would be the annotated program listing, together with a cross reference listing and an automatically drawn flowchart. Test data listings and test results would also be included, and the humanly produced documentation might simply be a high level flowchart or module hierarchy.

In order for this to be a satisfactory basis for program documentation, the coding standards need to be adhered to, and annotation should be very much better used than it commonly is; the odd comment here and there, with a few remarks at the beginning of the program, is just not sufficient. One must describe the purpose of the program and of each routine within it, and comments in the body of the coding should explain the reasons behind the actions. Use of switches should be explained, and comments should be mandatory at all branches.

The power of this method is that annotation is done during program writing, and there is no, or very little, human effort required on documentation after testing is over, in addition to which, of course, maintenance of the documentation becomes a machine activity. It is also possible, using this system, to utilise the machine to check whether documentation is being done according to standard, and, of course, such a program could also check on the coding standards used.

In short, then, documentation is a detested chore, and is therefore usually badly done. We maintain that it is sensible to automate it. If automation is not possible, the standards for documentation should still be high, and one way of enforcing them is for the maintenance section, if one exists, to refuse to take over a program until it is documented to standard.

.4.3   Performance standards

As explained above, performance standards are necessary in order to be able to estimate work and then to control it. Obviously one must ensure that a programmer cannot improve his performance simply by skimping on documentation, for instance: adequate checking of work, probably by senior programmers, is implied.

Programmer performance should, wherever possible, be made the basis of remuneration, but this implies extremely accurate estimating. However, the notion is a good one to bear in mind, and even if payment is not based directly on performance, the use of monthly 'league tables' based upon percentage performance can improve morale and competitiveness dramatically.

A basis often used for performance standards is that of so many statements per day, say 10 in Cobol, but we ourselves do not favour this method, preferring to break the tasks down into sub-tasks and then to estimate for each of these. The task method also has the advantage that it can be used for maintenance work as well as for initial development.

5.5 Opposition to programming standards

The creative aspects of a programmer's job are often given as a reason for opposing the introduction or use of programming standards. But we have also explained that standards can actually increase, rather than decrease, the creative side of the job, and they should therefore be sold on the basis that they provide a framework within which to use one's talent freely, rather than a straitjacket to restrict its use. In this way one can get over the creative hurdle. Commonly, however, the creative argument is simply a smokescreen to hide the real reasons for opposition—aversion to the discipline and control that the use of standards makes possible. This objection should be brought out into the open and shot down, using the 'being cruel to be kind' approach.

Any individual opposition can often be very effectively countered by co-opting the worst rebel onto the Standards Committee (see next section), which should exist to create the standards initially, and to review and update them thereafter.

5.6 Effectiveness

A poor standard that is used is infinitely more useful than a good standard that is not, but that is not a good reason for setting one's sights too low. One must decide on a level—perhaps a relatively low one in an established but standardless installation—put the standards in, and then aim to monitor, update, and improve upon them thereafter.

The major factor in enforcing standards is to have active involvement from the programmers using them, both when developing the standards initially and updating them afterwards. A Standards Committee should be set up to design the standards and to review them, and this committee should include rank and file members of the programming staff, possibly on a rotating basis. In this way the programmers feel committed to using the standards that they have helped to design.

6 Program design

The aim of Parts II and III of this book is to present work methods that have proven effective in minimising bugs and finding them quickly. The sequence of topics is that of program development. So far we have considered vital background areas such as staff recruitment and organisation, and work standards. Now we get down to development of a suite of programs and begin with the planning decisions that have to be taken.

Program design and the concept of 'building' a program are terms that have now almost completely taken over from the plain 'writing' of a program, and the use of these terms illustrates that engineering ideas and disciplines have now entered the programming sphere; in fact, that the systems engineering approach is being used. Broadly speaking, this approach says that a system or program should be treated like a piece of machinery, so that it should be smooth running, parts of it should be easily exchangeable, it should be easy to test, and so on. Its value lies in the emphasis it places on modularity, robustness and testability, and these are the three aspects of program design that this chapter covers.

But before one can design an individual program the suite must have been broken up, so we will look first at suite planning.

6.1 Suite planning

The decision on how to split up systems requirements into a good, efficient set of inter-connected programs is usually one taken jointly by systems analyst and senior programmer. Some installations attempt to make it the analyst's total responsibility but in general this implies the analyst having a strong programming background and can lead to a lowering of competence in the programming section. Others leave these decisions solely to the chief or senior programmer and, whilst this may lead to a good technical suite design, it may mean that some wide considerations are lost.

The basic requirement is to decide on the split of programs, taking into account both technical and systems constraints, including such matters as use of standard and installation software, etc.

There is often considerable external pressure to plunge headlong into the lengthy and unpredictable programming operation: management want to see results. This should be resisted and no programming started until the suite is fully designed and understood. Work commenced too soon may otherwise have to be scrapped or rehashed completely.

It is at this stage that tentative effort estimates can be produced for the programs within the suite and the whole operation scheduled.

To summarise, at this stage of development:

1. Programs have been identified and specified.
2. Tentative programming estimates have been made.
3. A schedule for programming exists.

6.2 Modular programming

6.2.1 Definitions

We devote considerable space later to discussion of the special problems that arise during testing in a modular programming environment and the special techniques that can be used. Our treatment at this point will only concern itself with the design implications: if modular programming is to be used we must know about it at the design stage. Programs will be split into modules, which will affect the plans for writing and testing, and will affect the number of staff required, target dates, etc.

All programmers nowadays adopt a modular approach to some degree: no one admits to writing large, monolithic programs. Perhaps, before going further, we had better describe the spectrum of possibilities and give our definition of modular programming:

(a) Monolithic: the program is written in one large block of coding and may only be compiled and tested as an entity; only one programmer can write it.

33

(b) Monolithic but of modular construction: the program is written as a number of defined subroutines (perhaps written by several people) with a short 'control program' which binds together the sections; the program may only be compiled as a whole but, by careful use of test aids (see later), could be tested routine by routine. We will call this approach 'modular-monolithic'.

(c) Modular: the program is written as a number of independent modules which are coded, compiled and tested individually, only being brought together to form the complete program when all are working independently. How the size and scope of modules are defined is a rather individual decision, which we will not discuss here. The comments are relevant using any (reasonable) criterion for module size.

6.2.2 Beneficial effects on debugging

When a program is broken down into smallish modules and each is specified separately, clearly more thought goes into the detailed design work and that can only be beneficial. In addition, smaller units mean less complexity, and so should be easier to test. Indeed it should be possible to test a module completely, i.e. every single logic path, which is usually impossible in a monolithic program of any size.

Because each module is tested independently, many can be in progress at once and can all be tested thoroughly before the complete program is linked. Although extra work is being done in splitting, interfacing, etc., the overall timescale can be dramatically shorter for a modular development.

Programmers writing modules tend to specialise and become language experts, input/output handling experts, etc. The increased proficiency can only result in fewer errors.

6.2.3 On the debit side

A vigorously enforced modular work-style *can* have the effect of producing one or two senior programmers in charge of a bevy of coders, who do little more than churn out simple modules as if on a production line. This is not desirable from a job satisfaction viewpoint and will lead to worthwhile programmers leaving. The remain-

34

ing staff will be less experienced and more error-prone. Of course, one of the major reasons for the 'invention' of modular programming was to reduce the skill required in programming. Taken too far, the effects are undesirable.

6.2.4 Conclusions

It is reasonable to say that there are no cast-iron arguments for or against modular programming. It is a subject on which people will argue passionately but our own feeling—having weighed up the arguments and seen it in action—is a neutral one. We are talking, of course, about a modular-monolithic technique compared with a thorough-going modular technique. There are advantages in program development achievable through both approaches and the violently modular approach *can* lead to staff problems if carried to extremes. A decision to 'go modular' should be based on a complete installation picture—existing staffing, type of programs developed, language, etc—and not just on the pros and cons of modular programming considered in the abstract.

It would be well to mention here that this book is aimed at all styles of programming and most topics are applicable to all. There are certain special problems that only arise during debugging in a modular environment and these are dealt with in a separate section (Part IV), but the rest of the book is applicable to a modular installation too.

6.3 Building a robust program

A robust program is like a large, amiable dog—not easily ruffled, slow to take offence and difficult to divert from its chosen course. Unfortunately most programs tend to be like toy poodles—very finicky about their food, demanding only the very best and tastiest tit-bits, very quick-tempered, easily upset and generally more trouble than they are worth.

Robustness derives from a number of sources, including sound coding techniques, good programming standards, a lack of naivety and stringent testing. The first point is partially included in the second and both are dealt with elsewhere (Chapters 7 and 5 respectively), but we shall extend the discussion here by briefly talking about what we have called pet programming techniques. The third source of robustness—lack of naivety—we split into two and call programming for errors and programming for amendments. The final point, on testing, is partially discussed here (building a testable program) and partially in Chapter 8.

6.3.1 Pet programming techniques

Pet programming techniques are really a programmer's own private set of standards, over and above any installation standards that may be present. They are standard ways of doing certain frequently encountered tasks such that the doing of the task becomes almost automatic—*and so less vulnerable to error*.

A programmer may have found in the past, for instance, that he was having trouble with iteration (looping) control, perhaps by varying the method to suit the values of existing constants (and so produce a more 'efficient' program). However, if he adopts a standard method—e.g. begin with count at zero; add 1 (or whatever) before comparison; compare with required number of iterations; return only if less—then he has a pet programming technique of his own, and he will benefit from its use.

Pet techniques are usually learned by either bitter experience or intelligent anticipation, but they are seldom passed on from one programmer to another. This seems a pity and we recommend that each installation tries to find out what pet techniques their programmers use, with a view to making their use at least semi-standard in the installation. We have found, however, that it is not as easy to discover pet techniques as it sounds; a round table discussion that we held with five or six very experienced programmers produced little of note, largely because it is not easy to bring pet techniques to mind in that sort of situation. So they are probably better gathered over a period of time by asking each programmer to jot down a note whenever he uses one of his own pet techniques during the course of his work.

6.3.2 Programming for errors

While it would be nice to live in a perfect world, the unfortunate fact

36

is that we do not and any programmer who thinks differently will probably not last very long. The programmer should take a rather jaundiced view of life and assume that his program has to survive all the sabotage attempts of cross-eyed punch girls, cretinous data control clerks, and idiotic operators.

The moral, therefore, is to assume that if anything can happen, it will; that things will go wrong rather than right, and to program accordingly.

On the other hand one must keep a sense of proportion because error checks can run away with both core and machine time. Never check for an error already checked by an earlier program in the suite and, for complicated checks, make some assessment of how often the error is likely to happen; a once-yearly failure of a daily program is probably acceptable, but a once-monthly failure is not.

Apart from checking for data errors, if they can occur, the following points are among the most important to remember when thinking about error checking.

File security

Most label checks are automatic these days, but never omit them on normal (i.e. standard) files. Be certain to have a back-up file before letting a new update program loose on a disc file.

Checkpoints

These are only necessary on long runs but should be in when they are needed. The operators must know the correct restart procedures.

Controls

Always generate batch and run controls. Valid and hash totals, transactions read and written, B/F and C/F master file figures are all used.

Operator errors

Reflect switch settings back to the operator and tell him what they mean; make him check them before continuing. Make operator messages meaningful. Take parameters from control cards, rather than from the console, wherever possible.

(The use of operating systems renders most of these points unnecessary if not impossible and the use of multi-programming usually places severe restrictions upon non-essential use of the console.)

Programmers should be told what to do on the above points—they should be part of the standards in any good installation.

6.3.3 Programming for amendments

It is a rare program that is never amended, and for this reason all programs should be written with an eye on ease of amendment. Simplicity and good documentation are essential if a program is to be at all easy to amend, but this ideal is still all too rarely found.

We have all sometimes, no doubt, struggled to amend a program and finally rewritten it in disgust. The good programmer's aim should be that none of his programs will ever be rewritten for this reason. The keys to ease of amendment are a well-structured program and the use of good programming standards, and we recommend that the chapter on programming standards be read again with amendments in mind, just to emphasise the point.

Since amending a program often means inserting more coding, or extra items in tables, one can simplify amendments by leaving space in tables, by always PERFORMING THRU (to allow for insertion of new paragraphs), by leaving gaps in sequence numbers and by keeping 'vital statistics' (e.g. table sizes) together as parameters, rather than scattered throughout the program as constants.

6.4 Building a testable program

Considering that every program must be tested before use and that almost every program contains errors when first written, it is difficult to understand why most programs are written on the assumption that they will work first time. Only two conclusions seem possible: professional programmers have an optimism bordering on naivety, or programming is still a very amateur occupation. The end result of either attitude is often a poorly tested program that gives continual trouble going live, that has errors cropping up throughout its life, and that may be so suspect that it is never run unless the programmer is on hand to sort out any difficulties.

The truly professional programmer programs with testing in mind, which means that he will:

(a) analyse the program for bug-prone areas, i.e. for complexities;
(b) decide which debugging aids to use and where and how to use them;
(c) program in these aids, to produce a testable program;
(d) test carefully with well-designed test data.

This will result in a program containing fewer errors, and these errors will be easier to find, so that the end result is a well-tested program in which every confidence can reside. Well-tested and confidence are key words here, for this sort of program gives little trouble going live and has a relatively trouble-free life.

6.4.1 Program complexity and testing implications

There is a programming aphorism that says that there are only three types of program—a validate, an update or a print. Like most such sayings it is not completely true, but it does contain more than a grain of truth. The point is that although every program is unique in terms of the details of the task, in principle it is performing one or more well-known functions.

From a testing point of view we can recognise three basic types of program complexity: file handling, arithmetic and logical. File handling complexity is really a type of logical complexity but has its own special problems, so is worth keeping separate. Most programs have a mixture of two or more types, but often one type will predominate, e.g. a major update program has mostly file handling complexity, a scientific or an invoicing program mostly arithmetic complexity and a data vet or information retrieval program mostly logical complexity.

Analysis of the program specification will show what types of complexity are present, and to what degree, and this allows the programmer to decide in advance the debugging aids he will use and pretty well how he will use them. The problems of debugging each type of complexity are standard and so the solutions can be pre-determined, as shown in Figure 6.1.

The diagram is largely self-explanatory and the way in which the debugging aids are used will be described later, but it is relevant here to comment that standard update logic is a pet technique rather than a debugging aid and that the mention of a slide-rule or desk calculator

Type of complexity	Testing problems	Applicable debugging aids
File handling	Test file creation File matching logic	Test data dispersion package Tape or disc print utilities (Standard update logic) Trace Snapshots
Arithmetic	Checking calculations	Snapshots (slide-rule or desk-calculator)
Logical	Loops and conditions (Robustness)	Trace Snapshots (object deck)

Fig. 6.1 Program complexity and testing implications

is somewhat light-hearted, though access to one can ease the work of the calculation or checking of results. The inclusion of an object deck ties in with robustness and implies that a data vet should never fail, so the final test should be with utter rubbish, e.g. an object deck.

6.4.2 Use of debugging aids

Chapter 3 described the types of debugging aid available to the programmer and this section will mainly consider the use of internal or programmed-in aids, i.e. snapshots and trace facilities.

Know your debugging aids

Debugging aids are the tools that a programmer uses to debug a program and, as with tools of any kind, they must be used in the correct place in the correct way to give good results. We have explained above how analysis of the program for complexities can show where to use particular aids, so now we have only to show how to use them in order to complete the picture.

But first let us look at how some programmers first use these programmed-in aids:

(a) The program is written with no debugging aids.

40

(b) On the first test the program goes wrong in some obscure way.

(c) The programmer looks up 'Debugging' in the manual, thinks a trace might be useful and puts it in at the beginning of the program.

(d) 24 hours and one test later, $1\frac{1}{2}$ boxes of printout come back.

(e) 'Blast! that trace was useless; I won't use that again' is the reaction.

And so once more a programmer, for lack of a little thought, is condemned to struggle unaided with his program debugging.

Characteristics of a good aid

A good programmed-in aid is flexible, can be conditioned and is easy to use. If your aids are not, then you can either program around them, e.g. condition them yourself, or write your own (as an installation, that is). For instance, a good snapshot will:

(a) identify its printout to show which bit of program it came from;

(b) be enabled or disabled by a particular condition, e.g. a switch setting;

(c) be flexible in terms of what it prints and the format of this printing.

How to use the aids: minimising the output

With either snapshots or trace, one must try to make the output significant but minimal, because otherwise faith, time and errors can all be lost. Loops present a particularly difficult problem here, particularly when they are nested, but there are two possible solutions.

Firstly one can minimise the number of passes through the loop by using careful and minimal early test data. For example, when searching a table for equality with a field from a record, the first test pack could consist of a two or three records only, each of which gives equality at or near the beginning of the table. This test would then have proved the logic of the loop except for getting out on inequality —which can be rigorously dry run, or will find itself later. Second and subsequent tests will have the debug print turned off for this part and will use more realistic data.

41

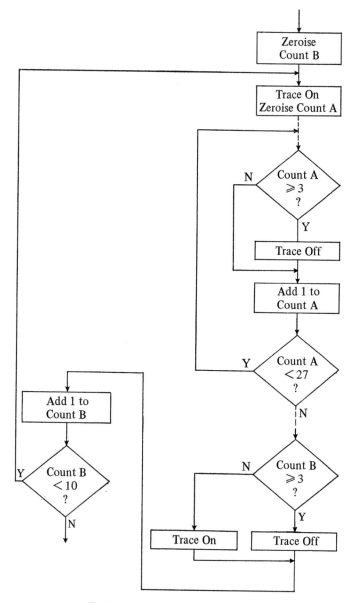

Fig. 6.2 Debugging prints in nested loops

Secondly one can turn off the debug print after two or three times through the loop. This tests the logic of the loop pretty thoroughly and is illustrated for a double loop in Figure 6.2. In this example each loop would give three sets of debug prints each time it is used and this will generally be adequate to debug them.

The trouble with trace

When the course of a program is being traced, one usually requires snapshots of control variables also, which most traces will not allow, so one often uses snapshots as a trace; this allows greater selectivity in the level of tracing, but requires more coding. Our own view is that snapshots are easier to use, more flexible and more useful than trace, so we concentrate on their use hereafter, although many of the principles are equally applicable to the use of trace.

Conditioning the output

The output from debug prints should always be conditioned, so that output from working parts of the program can be avoided. For example, a program containing a main loop and four subroutines, to be tested monolithically, might use five switches to control the output, one for the main loop and one for each subroutine.

Initially, all five switches will be on, but after each subroutine is proved its switch is turned off, to disable its output. Finally, for example during suite or system testing, all switches will be off.

What to print and when

The aim is to print just the information required to check both the final outputs from the program and the course and/or results of those parts of the program that analysis has revealed as bug-prone. Details are obviously very specific to a given program, but general guidance can be given. Whole examples of the use of some of the principles expounded will be found in Chapter 10.

(a) *Input and output records*
  The input is usually printed by a utility before testing and output to anything but the printer is normally printed by a utility after each test.

Printed output is generally left to speak for itself, but if any complicated printing is to be done it may be worthwhile to print the output by a snapshot before entering the print routine (and a trace may also be put in the print routine itself).

(b) *Tracing*

Tracing debugs logic, so one is interested in branching and its control and for this reason a snapshot before each important branch to print the values of the control variables at that point will fill the bill (Figure 6.3).

(c) *Snapshots*

Snapshots, used normally (i.e. not for tracing), are mostly used to print arithmetic values in order to check the course of a calculation. For short calculations, a print of the answer(s) and input(s) (if they were program-generated) will be sufficient, but in a longer calculation the values of intermediate results will also be required.

(d) *Post-mortem dumps*

A dump is often requested in the event of a program failure, endless looping, crazy printing, etc. On the IBM 360/370 in particular, dumps are designed as a debugging aid, so they are helpful and easily understood, whereas the dumps on most machines are not too helpful and a lot of time can be wasted with them.

In general, we are very much against the use of dumps, because they encourage programmers to begin debugging only when an error occurs: we repeat that the output from a well-written program, with snapshots in at all the right spots, will contain, in conjunction with the source, input and output listings (if any) all the information needed to find the bug.

Two other powerful arguments against the use of dumps are that they tempt the programmer to correct only the run-stopping error, whereas he should always check all the output; and dumps are in machine language, whereas most programmers program in high-level languages these days.

What to do with them afterwards

Debug prints will usually be left in the program through suite and system testing and probably parallel running also, only being removed when the program goes into production.

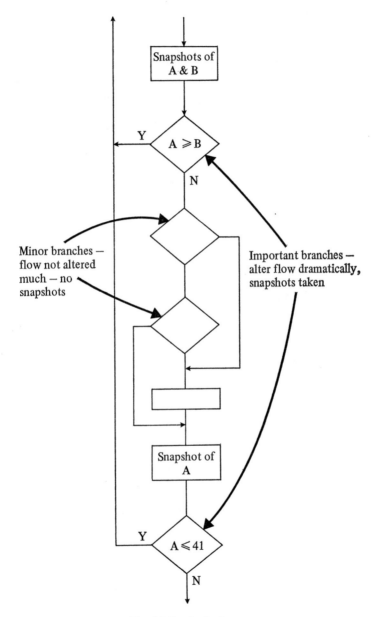

Fig. 6.3 Tracing logic

6.5 Design expression

The final program design is almost always expressed in flowchart form, though the use of decision tables is becoming more common.

It is debatable where during program design bug avoidance ends and bug identification begins, but we will take an arbitrary decision and say that bug identification begins with the flowchart, which is therefore the first topic dealt with in Part III.

Part III Bug identification and elimination

7 Program writing

In this chapter we intend to cover the stages in program development between the end of program planning and the first actual test. The placing of this chapter at the beginning of the main section on bug identification and elimination is highly indicative of our philosophy: up to this stage it is possible to take reasonable steps to avoid or minimise the incidence of bugs, but as soon as pencil is actually put to paper to write the program, bugs begin to appear. There are certain ways of writing a program that are clearly less error-prone; there are certain steps that can be taken to find and eliminate errors before the program ever reaches the machine; these we shall consider here.

We firmly believe that a programmer taking extra care and certain precautions at this stage will save a great deal of his own time as well as machine-time later: pithily, cheap time now saves expensive time later. Occasions do arise however where machine time is cheaper than manpower, for example in the use of 'expensive' consultants or if the penalty for not completing a program to a very close deadline is high. In this kind of circumstance obviously a different approach to the relative duration of stages in program development should be made. In general, though, extra time spent now will more than pay for itself in saved programmer and machine time later.

The stages to be discussed here are flowcharting, test planning, coding, desk checking, dry-running and test data design. There is no magic way of performing these operations to render them foolproof: few of the ideas we suggest could be termed original but they do need bringing up again and stressing. Doing these things in a methodical, even formalised, way is the only means of achieving programs of reasonable quality when they reach the machine for the first time.

47

7.1 Flowcharting

7.1.1 Purpose

The object of flowcharting at this stage in program development (as opposed to flowcharting for documentation purposes later) is to 'crack' the basic problem presented by the specification and express it, however broadly at first, in terms of valid programmable procedures. Most programmers produce a very rough flowchart at this stage, indeed usually a hierarchy of them, each nearer to the final solution than the last. Often these would be incomprehensible to anyone else because most programmers have a sort of personal flowcharting convention for use in these initial charts. The object is to translate on to paper as rapidly as possible, and before forgotten, the basic ideas on program structure that flash through the mind. It is not usually feasible, therefore, that these initial charts should be neat or even involve the use of a template: neatness would slow down the flow of ideas on to paper. The neat flowchart comes later and for a different purpose.

There is quite a strong tendency for a programmer to regard flowcharting as a rather trivial preliminary to 'programming' itself, i.e. coding. An extremely sketchy and ill-thought-out scribble often serves as the coding guide. This is wrong. It is worth taking a little extra time to do the job properly: an error in the flowchart is an error in the basic structure of the program and recovery from it can be difficult, time consuming and expensive.

7.1.2 Levels and structure

There are many levels of flowchart, from the very broad one describing where the whole computer system fits into the business environment to the very detailed, one-box-per-statement type showing program mechanics and flow. Each level could have a purpose but only three are generally used at the program stage:

- (a) the general, 'external' flowchart in problem-orientated terms, used to give a quick understanding of what the program does;
- (b) the macro-flowchart showing program structure at a glance;
- (c) the detailed micro-flowchart: the coding guide, normally at 'routine' level.

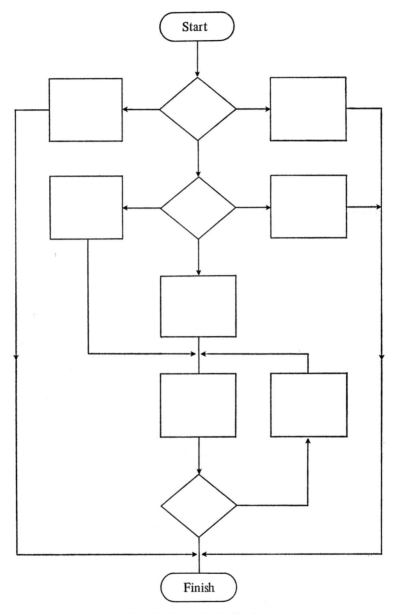

Fig. 7.1 Pictorial-style flowchart

The structure of flowcharts tends to reflect the structure of the program, or vice versa, the two main alternatives being monolithic and modular. A monolithic flowchart is written as one long stream for page after page, with many interpage and off-page connectors. It is difficult to draw and very difficult to follow.

A modular flowchart consists of an overall flowchart defining the program structure and then detailed charts describing each single function in the main structure. Modular as against monolithic program construction is discussed elsewhere in this book: suffice it to say at this point that, in flowcharting too, both techniques can be inefficient and error-prone if carried to excess.

7.1.3 Method of construction

Style

There are two principal, mutually exclusive methods, each of which has advantages over the other. Most installations have some standards dictating which style of chart is preferred.

Figure 7.1 shows a 'pictorial' style flowchart. It is fully two-dimensional and represents the problem structure more closely than it represents the actual coding of the program. It is much easier to grasp the logical structure of the program from such a chart and most programmers' initial scribbles are of this style.

The other style—flowchart in code order—is illustrated in Figure 7.2. This is one-dimensional and follows the coding closely. Whilst it would be easier to code from this style of flowchart, it is more difficult to draw before coding. Flowcharts produced from the coding after development for documentation purposes, whether manually or by automatic flowcharting packages, tend to be of this type.

Debugging aids

When internal debugging aids are being used (as discussed in Chapter 6), a detailed flowchart should show where and how the aids are to be used. For example, if a snapshot print is to be included, the flowchart must show:

    (a) where it is used;
    (b) what identification is to be printed;

(c) what switch or conditions control printing;

(d) what is to be printed.

It is an important principle that these things should be decided and written down *before* coding: a programmer several days into coding a complex program and encountering a point for a snapshot-print does not want to be distracted by thinking about how to identify the print, etc.

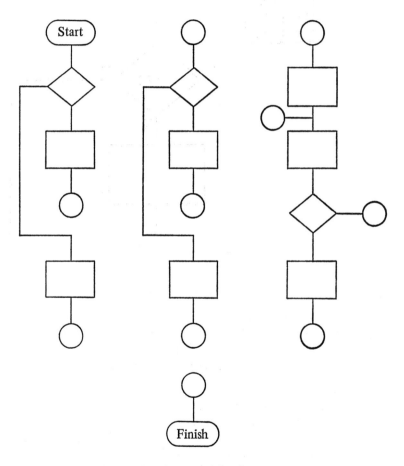

Fig. 7.2 One-dimensional flowchart

51

Figure 7.3 shows how the notes can be added simply to a flowchart without cluttering it.

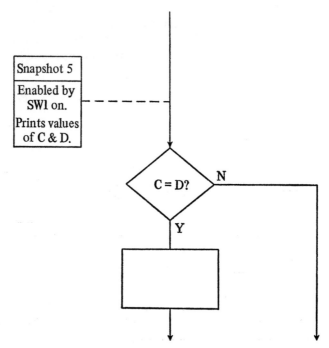

Fig. 7.3 Snapshot print included in flowchart

7.1.4 Common errors in flowcharting

It is worth mentioning some of the more common errors made in flowcharting. This is not an exhaustive list and the reader may wish to add some points of his own: it could then form a useful checklist for dry running the flowchart before coding.

1. Confusion of two paths leaving a decision box.
2. Missing a logical path completely.
3. Linkage to and from subroutines.
4. Confusion in representing loops, especially nested ones.
5. Failure to dry run flowchart before coding.
6. Failure to understand the problem—bad liaison with analyst.

7.1.5 The role of the flowchart

As mentioned earlier, there are two principal reasons for flowcharting. In the first instance, the programmer's ideas on program structure and content must be put down on paper to provide a guide during coding and subsequent testing. This can be informal, even freehand; as long as the programmer himself can use it, that is enough. When testing is over and the job complete, a neat, easily understood flowchart is required for documentation purposes; we have already discussed this task in Chapter 5.

7.2 The test plan

7.2.1 Purpose

We have found from our own experience that the drawing up of a document which we call the Test Plan is extremely helpful in making the debugging process more efficient. It is an idea that any programmer can try for himself (with no costly overheads) and we recommend its use highly to the reader. But what *is* it?

Basically, and rather in generalities, it is a strategic plan of how to test the program concerned as quickly and comprehensively as possible. One of the major factors contributing to poor debugging is inflexibility of approach: a complex file update is tested using similar strategy to a simple card validation. We recognise that programs do fall into a number of general categories but each one tends to be in a different complexity/data environment and deserves a different strategy for testing it. The Test Plan enables the programmer to recognise this and vary his approach.

The simple process of writing a Test Plan down is its most important point: it forces a programmer to think and makes him look ahead and anticipate its testing problems.

7.2.2 When prepared

The best time to prepare the Test Plan is after the initial flowcharting, because the main program structure is then known and the problems of testing can be examined before the details confuse the issue.

53

7.2.3 Contents

What we have said about the Test Plan so far is rather general but we have included a specific example (for the case study program developed later in the book—see page 96) which, perhaps, ought to be consulted as we list the components:

(a) General strategy: a general outline of the testing programme and thoughts on problems that might arise and their solution.

(b) Module testing strategy: if appropriate, this will be concerned with use of testing packages, order of testing, methods of testing particular modules, module link testing, etc.

(c) Input data: how test files are to be created, including notes on the use of packages, utilities or the need to write special one-off programs.

(d) Use of test aids: as discussed earlier.

(e) Expected results schedule: this can only be drawn up after the test data has been designed and sometimes only after the program has been written. It consists of a list of results that should be obtained from the test data used. Such schedules are tedious to do but need not be done minutely: a middle course suggested is to calculate the answers and totals but not to write down output formats in detail. It is important that at least one output of each type is specified beforehand so that general formats can be checked after the test. This schedule must be drawn up and added to the Test Plan before testing begins. It will be mentioned again later.

7.3 Coding

In Chapter 5 we talked of the importance of adhering to good programming standards, but even if this is done coding errors will still be introduced and it is fair to say that most program errors are introduced during coding.

7.3.1 Common errors

Irrespective of language used, there are certain errors that occur over and over again and are worth mentioning. All programmers have 'blind spots': certain mistakes they make time and again. We will be mentioning these and how to combat them shortly, but it is worth giving now our (necessarily incomplete) list of the most common coding errors. Note that this list is language-independent.

1. Omission in coding of one or more flowchart/decision table boxes.
2. Improper or omitted address modification.
3. Reference to undefined symbols.
4. Multi-defined symbols/datanames.
5. Transcription of the characters in a dataname.
6. Not initialising counters or accumulators.
7. Failure to save and/or restore registers.
8. Absolute addresses left unchanged after program modification.
9. Incorrect format of statements.
10. Incorrect calling of subroutines.
11. Failure to set and/or reset switches.
12. Creation of endless loops.
13. Overwriting of constants.
14. Incorrect use of a base system.
15. Failure to allow for accumulator overflow.
16. Ignoring overflow or carry.
17. Wrong branches.
18. Improper termination of loops.
19. Wrong number of loop cycles.
20. Improper or omitted loop initialisation.
21. Failure to open and/or close files.
22. Failure to clear print lines.
23. Failure to consult manual if in doubt.

7.3.2 Coding method

It is interesting to note that the structure of the typical Cobol program is a near-perfect methodology for the coding process generally, whatever language is being employed. Its divisional structure, both in content and order, makes the programmer build up the program in a highly logical way—a way designed to minimise errors.

First of all, it says, identify the program in some way and note its purpose; then state the hardware environment in which it is intended to run; then define the data to be manipulated. (A useful time and error saver here is the use of the same file and/or record specifications in each program using them. Even manually this can be done quite simply by, for instance, using photocopied versions of the one set of coding, while facilities are built into most languages to allow it to be done automatically, e.g. COPY in Cobol and macro facilities in PL/1 and most assembly languages.)

Then define constants, accumulators, counts, subscripts, work areas and switches. Usually this is done as coding progresses but an attempt should be made to keep similar items together and allow room for later insertions.

Now write the actual procedure instructions, keeping them as easy to understand as possible. They will then be easier to test and amend later. Whatever comment facilities are available in the language should be used liberally. A few meaningful comments can make even the most complex routine readily understandable. It is important that comments should be more than just a 'running commentary' on what the instructions are doing: they must say *why* as well as *how*. Comments should always be placed in a common position, either before or after the coding to which they refer. Debugging aids should be incorporated at the points decided earlier.

7.3.3 Precautions against errors

The rest of this section we devote to dos and don'ts: most of them are well known but nevertheless important.

Always aim to use meaningful labels and datanames. This is not difficult in most high level languages but it is surprising the number of programmers who use highly abbreviated labels simply to save writing effort.

Avoid using the same data area for several unrelated purposes—it can lead to endless confusion and there is no real argument for it unless core store is severely restricted.

A close check should be kept on 'global' variable names when more than one programmer is involved. Either a unique first letter can be assigned to each programmer or a master list of variables can be maintained, new ones being checked against it before use.

All loops and areas of complex coding should be dry run immediately after coding.

Check all subroutine calling sequences and parameter lists: an out-of-order parameter list can cause some very difficult-to-find bugs later.

Tick off each flowchart box as it is coded to avoid duplication or omission. These faults are extremely common and easy to make, especially if the coding is spread over several days.

Sequence the coding to allow for changes or insertions. In addition to its obvious use, the sequence number can be used to identify segments of the program by allocating easily distinguishable blocks of numbers to each.

To summarise: there is no guaranteed way of producing bug-free code; a methodical approach and application of the points mentioned above will help, though.

7.4 Desk checking

The detailed checking of a program before it leaves the programmer's desk is a vital process if a prolonged testing session on the machine is to be avoided. Everyone likes to have a 'clean' compilation but we would go so far as to say that every compilation *ought* to be clean. The programmer should not be content to let the compiler do his work. If the machine time is available, it is usually better to get a straight listing of the punched source code. This should show any punching errors and make the checking easier than working from coding sheets. A simple listing will be a lot quicker than a compilation for this purpose.

7.4.1 Syntax checklists

Desk checking mainly finds syntax errors in the coding and we have found that checklists of common errors in the language concerned are useful to read as 'reminders' before commencing the actual check and we would suggest that installations draw up their own.

7.4.2 Error search

This should be a systematic process. A suggested method is:

1. Check branches: look for faulty logic, spelling mistakes in labels, missing conditions.
2. Sending fields or variables referenced: check for spelling mistakes, invalid formats, wrong values, omission of initialisation.
3. Receiving fields or variables set by assignment: again check for spelling mistakes, also for invalid formats. Beware of undetected overflow.
4. Check and re-check all conditional tests: disagreement with field definitions, invalid logical expressions, etc. Keep logical expressions simple to avoid trouble.
5. Check literals and constants for invalid formats, duplication, etc.
6. Check punctuation carefully: omission of essential punctuation or insertion of extra items can cause trouble.

If feasible, we suggest as a final effort that another programmer scans the program for obvious errors: what strikes his attention may have escaped the author's.

7.5 Dry running

7.5.1 Definition

Dry running means manual checking of a program with simple test data, simulating the passage of the data through it. It is very useful in finding logic errors, as desk checking is in finding syntax errors. It ought to be an essential phase of programming, but how many programmers really do it? It can be a tedious process but if approached in the right way need not be.

7.5.2 Method

Better and quicker results are achieved with two persons participating, and then the process is also less tedious. The method is simple: one person pretends he is the central processor obeying the program while the other person records data fields, passing information to the 'processor' and receiving results back. The process allows the programmers to become extremely familiar with the logic of the program and can save a lot of otherwise wasted early tests on the machine.

7.6 Test data

Test data is most commonly designed at this point, i.e. when the program is being punched, and we want to look in detail at the importance of good program test data and its design. But first we will very briefly consider the types of test data and the levels of testing that a program must live through before finally being pronounced clean.

.6.1 Test data provision

There are three principal types of test data:

(a) *Programmer data.* This tests the program as the programmer sees fit and it only tests what he has written. It will not find errors of interpretation of specs., nor will it test sections of program accidentally omitted by the programmer. It should, on the other hand, test every program path at least once and main paths exhaustively. Programmer data is usually fairly limited in volume and often does not test all error possibilities. We will look at its design in detail below.

(b) *Analyst data.* This tests the suite of programs and ensures that the analyst's intentions have been satisfied. It is probably not much like 'live' data because the transaction ratios, error rates, etc., will be distorted to test error conditions. It will try to check nearly as much as the programmer's data and will be similar in terms of volume.

(c) *User data.* This tests the system as a whole to ensure that it does what the user expects. Usually it is actual, realistic data, often historical, having the normal transaction proportions and the expected ratios of errors to valid transactions. Because of this it principally tests the main logic paths and the more obscure errors not at all, unless special test transactions are included. Volumes are normally realistic and the run time estimates can be checked for the first time.

.6.2 Testing levels

(a) *Stand-alone testing* is when a programmer tests his program or module individually, using data he has created himself, to sort out logic errors, etc.

(b) *Link-testing* is the testing of the links between individual modules within a program, or programs within a suite, checking relationships and interfaces as much as final output.

(c) *Systems testing* aims to test a complete suite of programs and also the user department. It gives the user practice in using the system and should find any remaining snags.

(d) *Parallel running* is a final check using live data to verify the accuracy of the system and to give confidence to the user.

(e) *Live running* is not, strictly speaking, a phase of testing, but is unfortunately regarded as such in some installations!

7.6.3 Design of programmer test data

We have no sympathy at all with those programmers who do not test their programs with good and comprehensive test data, and we would have no compunction about sacking such a programmer.

Designing test data is a longish job, but it should not be particularly boring, because it is a task that requires a good deal of imagination. The best way to tackle it is, as always, to work in a methodical fashion, which will minimise the chances of missing anything.

First of all one should write down the separate file conditions that need to be included, so that each file used will contain all significant combinations. One might have, for instance, a file containing groups of records, each group consisting of a header record and a variable number of detail records, and it might be that a group could contain either a lone header record or a header record with any combination of detail records. In this case one would want to have lone header groups, both singly and together, groups with all detail records, groups without the first detail record or without the last, or without either, groups with gaps in the middle, and so on, depending on the requirements of the file. The transaction file that updates this group file would need one record per group, several records per group, different transaction types, and so on.

Next the conditions that can arise when the two files are enmeshed should be written down: unmatched masters, unmatched transactions, updating of existing detail records, insertion of new detail records at the beginning, middle and end of a group, insertion of two

60

Master File	Transactions File	Condition
Part code 1	—	Unmatched master
—	Part code 2 insertion	Unmatched trans. to be inserted
Part code 4	Part code 4 update	Update
Part code 5	Part code 5 deletion	Deletion
etc.	etc.	etc.

Fig. 7.4 File-matching conditions

consecutive detail records, updating of a newly inserted detail record should all be catered for, and more.

Finally, the program should be examined, and important conditions to test added to this list. These will include boundary conditions, special values of fields that cause particular actions, error conditions, end of file conditions, and a whole lot more.

The completed list then forms the best possible basis for designing test data, and data can now be put together that will satisfy these conditions. It is of great value to write the data down in a schematic way at first, giving against each record (or record combination in the case of running files against one another) a note of what conditions are being tested. Figure 7.4 gives the beginning of such a schematic for an update.

As each condition is included it can be ticked off, until eventually the schematic will contain all required conditions.

The schematic now acts as the input to the actual generation of test data records and also acts as a form of expected results schedule, so that two big birds are killed with the one reasonably small stone.

7.7 Job control

As operating systems become more sophisticated and complex, they form yet another barrier between the programmer and the machine Using them becomes yet another error-prone operation the programmer has to master. All prior efforts can be spoiled by not having the same professional approach to job control.

Such errors are extremely common: we must all have come across the program that takes six attempts just to be compiled and executed —because of job control problems. Use of 'catalogued' or library procedure facilities will help and should be used whenever possible.

Always get a second opinion if in doubt on job control: being forced to explain one's requirements often results in spotting errors or omissions. Some larger installations even go so far as to remove the problem from the programmer and set up specialist job control teams who do nothing else but that. Whilst being indicative of a hardly ideal state of affairs in software, the idea is to be recommended

8 Program testing

In this chapter we will take our coats off and get down to talking about how to test programs. In particular we will examine the usual method of testing and isolate its defects, and from those defects we will define the requirements of a better method. Finally we will describe a method that we have used and that fulfills all our requirements for a better method.

But first we will mention the documentation of the efforts made by a programmer to test his program.

8.1 The program development log

.1.1 Purpose

The idea behind this document is to present a blow-by-blow account of progress—or lack of it—right through the development of a program, but particularly during testing, so that each test and its results are documented.

The log is extremely useful to the programmer when he is asked to report progress, and in fact it can form the basic input document to a programming project control system. It also serves to remind the programmer of precisely where he is, which is easy to get confused about when working on several programs at a time, and it can also pinpoint reasons for delay: poor turnround on punching or testing, for example.

An important point about the use of a log is quite a simple one: if one is forced to write something about one's errors, there is a strong incentive to be more careful, to avoid entries like 'failed—incorrect job control', for instance. This aspect is reinforced if, as we recommend, the logs are retained by the Programming Manager at the end of testing.

PROGRAMMER A. Jones	PROGRAM NO. BD 019	PROGRAM NAME Stock update		SYSTEM Stock control 1 of 7			
						TIME TAKEN	
EVENT OR ACTIVITY	DATE OR DATES	ACTION OR RESULTS		NEXT STEP	MAN (DAYS)	M/C (MINS)	
Received spec.	1•4•71	Set aside for present		Study spec.	—	—	
Study spec.	5•4•71 to 7•4•71	Raised 3 queries with analyst. His memo to me of 9•4•71 refers		Modularisation	2½	—	

Fig. 8.1 Sample program development log

64

But possibly the most useful purpose of such a log is to help the programmer improve his performance by critically reviewing the log at the end of the job, ideally with his superior. In this way strong points are recognised, and weak points can be isolated for attention. This review is of great importance and should not be skimped, as it can provide senior programmers with both an objective view of the work of the programmer and a chance to discuss the programmer's work with him.

The final use of the log is as an input to the estimating process: actual times taken can be compared with the estimates, and the reasons for any discrepancies may be clear from the log. On the other hand, the comparison may well indicate consistent over or under-estimating for particular phases, e.g. coding.

8.1.2 Contents

An example of a partially completed log is shown in Figure 8.1 and an example of an actual log is shown in Appendix 8. It can be seen that the relatively free format of the log allows its use to be abused by filling in as little as possible. Any tendency of this nature can easily be counteracted, however, and programmers should be encouraged to use the log almost as a daily diary; certainly any significant point should be on there. As with most things, the more effort that is put into the keeping of the log, the more use it will be to all concerned.

8.2 Usual testing method

8.2.1 Pre-test planning

As already explained, most programmers write programs on the assumption that they will either work first time or that any errors will be easy to find and correct. This will almost certainly have led to the building of a program that is not particularly testable.

In addition to this, desk checking and dry running will generally have been skimped, with the result that the first two or three tests might fail because of some trivial errors that are easy to spot and correct. This might well, in a perverse sort of way, support the notion that the program will be easy to test.

65

8.2.2 Examination of test results

It is almost universally true that examination of test results is not thorough enough. The lack of a good expected results schedule, combined with a feverish desire to get the program back in for the next test, inevitably means that some errors are not spotted at all, or are only spotted on a later test, thus wasting time and tests.

Very often the worst thing that can happen from the point of view of checking test results is that the program should fail, because attention is immediately concentrated upon the failure and the reason for it, with an almost complete neglect of the other, equally valid and useful, results.

There is another unofficial index of performance that postulates that the faster a test is turned round and put back in, the better the programmer. Nothing could be further from the truth: the frenetic searching of dumps, pulling at beards, and punching of cards is a recipe for disaster and should be positively sought out and stamped out. It is useful in this context to limit programmers to a single test on any one program per day, giving a powerful incentive to reduce the number of test shots taken.

8.2.3 Finding causes of errors and correcting them

This is the saddest area of all.

Finding the cause of those errors that a programmer has been lucky enough to spot is usually a very haphazard business that will often involve theorising about causes right from the start. Yet another unofficial index of performance has it that a programmer who cannot immediately come up with a theory about the cause of an error is no programmer at all, and the trouble is that many programmers believe so implicitly in their ability to do this that they act on their theory without checking it out. In short, then, the 'correction' of errors is based more on inspired guesswork, experience, and hunches than on solid fact, and this easily leads to correction of only part of an error, or even to going backward rather than forward.

8.2.4 Stubborn errors

Even so, there are sometimes errors that baffle even the best theoriser, and in this case it is common to see debugging aids inserted in a

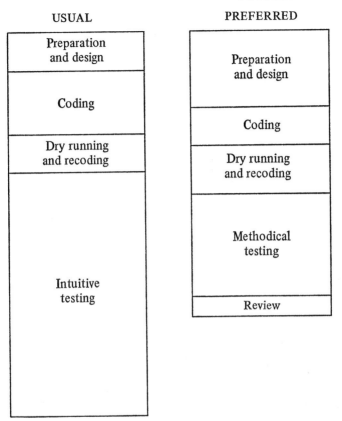

USUAL   PREFERRED

Fig. 8.2 Program development timescales—usual and preferred

hurry, and so without much thought, and this can lead to the disillusionment described in Chapter 6. Another popular method of trying to resolve a difficult error is to discuss it with another programmer, and it is surprising how often it happens that while describing the error to someone else the reason for it becomes plain.

8.3 Faults of usual testing method

The main fault is that of inefficiency: the use of experienced guesses

67

is by no means bad, in fact it is sometimes the only way, but the inefficiency lies in using the experience with little guidance as to where and how it is to be applied.

The use of an inefficient process causes testing to be much slower than it should be.

But most important of all, testing is often not comprehensive and thorough enough, and this, linked with poor test data, can easily lead to a poorly tested, troublesome program.

8.4 Requirements of a better method

Bugs must be anticipated and debugging aids used in order to find them if they do occur. This was covered in Chapter 6.

The information that careful planning and programming has produced must be used efficiently in order to:

(a) recognise errors;
(b) find the causes of these errors;
(c) amend efficiently and correctly;
(d) debug the amendments, to ensure that they correct the errors and do not produce further errors.

A method that can fulfil these requirements should affect programming time scales as shown in Figure 8.2. This diagram implies that the better method should spend more time on planning, but less on testing, and less overall.

8.5 A better method described

8.5.1 Recognition of errors

Errors can only be recognised by examining test results for deviations from what was expected from that test. These deviations can be major ones like failing to open a file, for instance, or they can be relatively minor ones like an incorrect total. But the fact that errors can only be found and corrected by first recognising their effects suggests at least two things:

(a) the programmer must know the expected results of the tests;

(b) the test data must be good and comprehensive.

These two points are fundamental to the recognition of errors but they are all too often forgotten, and even if they are not forgotten, the effort of producing a good expected results schedule and of designing first class test data is often too great. A methodical way of doing both was described in Chapter 7.

In an ideal world, where the test data contained all relevant conditions, and where the program was written sufficiently well that each piece of input data produced some (right or wrong) recognisable results, it would be sufficient simply to check the output against the expected results schedule and all deviations would be discovered. But unfortunately these conditions do not often apply, and so the program will usually need to contain debug prints to monitor the course of the program. Intelligent use of these prints will allow one to approach the ideal much more closely.

The output from the first one or two tests, which probably did not go through to the end, and which probably used shorter and simpler test files, will be checked very thoroughly indeed. One can trace the processing performed on each input record by utilising the source listing, the debug prints (all of which will be turned on), any other printed output, any output file listings, and the expected results schedule. In this way one will validate the workings of the most important parts of the program. In addition, it will generally be the case that programming errors will be spotted here that would not normally be spotted until the later, more complicated tests, so possibly saving one or two tests.

Even if one or more of these first tests does not get as far as printing a line, or writing a record, or whatever, the insertion and checking of debug prints will salvage a lot more from the tests by allowing the processing up to the failure point to be checked out, whereas normally the test would only yield the reason for the failure.

The information gained by this careful checking will enable some parts of the program to be checked out quite early, and their debug prints may then be turned off. In other cases one will be reasonably sure of the workings of the program, but will prefer to leave the debug prints on, not to go right through them every time, necessarily, but as back-up when the ordinary output indicates a fault in that area. So, in later tests, using larger and more complicated test files, one will simply check the overt results against those expected.

There is only one final point to be made here: make quite sure that a deviation between expected and actual results is a real one; in other words check the expected results schedule carefully against the data to see if the expected result is really that. Otherwise one can spend many fruitless and unhappy hours searching for an error that just does not exist.

8.5.2 Finding the causes of errors

If the program has been written in the way that we have suggested, and if it is tested as described above, then causes of errors will be found very simply. Either the incorrect processing is found before the deviation in the expected results—the cause found before the symptom, in other words—or else the deviation is found and the debug prints can be used to find the cause fairly easily. But programs are not always written and tested as we suggest, and one does not always have debug prints in at all the right places, or on at the right time, and so one is sometimes stuck with a deviation and no clear direction in which to look for a cause. In this situation the need is for a method that will provide clues to the area in which to look for the cause, and that will enable the cause found to be verified as the complete and correct one.

We will describe and illustrate such a method (we call it 'The Method') in the next chapter, because it deserves space to itself, but before then we want to complete the rest of the stages in the cycle of finding and correcting errors.

8.5.3 Program amendments

Once the cause of an error has been found, the error must then be eliminated, and this correction should be treated as though it is a program in itself. All reasonable ways of performing the task should be considered, a 'best' one chosen, and the debugging problems of the new coding should be considered and any required debugging aids inserted. And finally the coding should be desk checked and dry run, the test data altered to test it out (if necessary), and the expected results schedule altered if it will be affected.

Of course, the amendment will be that much easier to make if the program has been written with amendment in mind, as described earlier. The actual insertion of the coding into the source program will be done in one of the ways described in Chapter 3, or possibly manually in the case of a source deck of cards.

Whilst on the subject of program amendment, we should mention program maintenance once again. Because it involves operational programs, program maintenance must be done extremely carefully, and all amendments checked very thoroughly, and so all of our remarks above apply to this activity also, but with far greater force.

We have mentioned the staffing problems of program maintenance in Chapter 4 and the only other feature worthy of note is that of security. Most installations have a way of distinguishing between testing and operational versions of programs and files simply in order that a testing version of a program is never let loose on an operational system. Thus, when a program needs maintenance, a testing copy of the source is taken, and this is amended, tested, system checked and cleared for use, and it is then phased in, as an operational program, in place of the old version, which will then probably be used as a back-up in case of failure of the maintained version. In some cases, of course, the old version will still be required as an operational program, and here the two will probably be distinguished by number.

A deeper discussion of program maintenance would be out of place in this book, because we are discussing initial program development and the easing of the maintenance task, but not the performance of maintenance work in itself.

9 The Method

In this chapter we describe what we have come to call 'The Method'.

The Method has usually been one of the most controversial features of our discussions on debugging, but it was not introduced simply to provide useful discussion: although it is controversial we feel it has a part to play. It is in fact an adaptation of a problem-solving technique developed by Kepner & Tregoe* for use by managers.

9.1 The place of The Method

Figure 9.1 shows that, out of six possible areas in which The Method could be used, in one only is the use of it (or something akin to it) not required. The exception is usually cause finding while testing a well-planned program, when (as we saw in Chapter 8) incorrect processing and its later consequences are relatively easy to find. In the same chapter we also saw that verification of such errors is usually straight-forward enough, but nevertheless The Method does have a role to play here, and we will see how when we look at the testing of the case study program.

The Method really comes into its own in situations when one is simply faced with a deviation that has to be put right—commonly in a hurry. The worst example of this is a production fault when, in the middle of a reel of tape, perhaps, and probably in the middle of the night too, the program fails. The operator may or may not notice anything, and the job may or may not get thrown off, but whatever the situation the programmer is faced with a fault, some scanty information about it, and possibly someone important breathing down his neck, waiting for him to come up with the answer—fast.

In this situation the programmer must make the best of a bad job,

*Kepner, C. H., & Tregoe, B. B. *The Rational Manager*, McGraw-Hill, 1965.

Situation	Cause Finding	Cause Verification
Well-planned program Normal testing	✗	✓
Badly-planned program Normal testing	✓	✓
Unexpected or difficult errors during testing	✓	✓
Production faults Crisis situations	✓	✓

Fig. 9.1 The place of The Method

and that means using all of the information he is given, or can discover, to find and verify the cause of the deviation.

9.2 What The Method does

In the situation just described the programmer concerned must, knowingly or unknowingly, critically examine and evaluate the information he has and then use the results of this examination as a source of inspiration as to which area of the program contains the error. The Method offers him a way of formalising, and of bringing into the light of day, this process. In a nutshell, it guides his search for information by telling him what to look for, and gives him a powerful means of analysing this information in order to pinpoint the area of the program in which the error lies. And finally, it makes it easy for him to verify that the cause found is the complete and correct one.

Information collected under four headings

?	IS	IS NOT
WHAT		
WHEN		
WHERE		
TO WHAT EXTENT		

Distinctions

↓

Hypotheses

↓

Causes

Fig. 9.2 Bug analysis grid

9.3 The Method described

9.3.1 Specification of the deviation

The basis of The Method is to define the deviation that has been found, and it is from this definition, or specification, that all else flows. Figure 9.2 shows the headings that are used.

With these headings in mind, one first gathers information and pigeonholes it into the appropriate slots, and if any particular slot seems sparsely filled then the search for information can be intensified in that area. This structuring and guiding of the search for information is of great help in a task that is usually a very hit-and-miss affair.

The splitting of the specification into IS and IS NOT sides is the unique and vital part of The Method, because it is the presence of clear distinctions between the two sides that provides the clues as to the cause of the deviation. Unfortunately, a beginner finds it rather difficult at first, probably because he is too used to looking for similarities, rather than differences. However, it is something that one gets better at with a little practice, and we shall soon be seeing some examples of the art.

9.3.2   Look for distinctions

Once the information has been pigeonholed, each part of the specification is examined to see if there is any distinction between the IS and IS NOT sides. This is absolutely vital, because if the circumstances or conditions under which a fault does not happen are sharply differentiated from those under which it does happen, then we can pinpoint the most likely areas of the program for the error. For instance, if the fault occurs when processing record type A, but not when processing record type B, then we can say quite definitely that there *must* be something different between the processing of the two record types, and that the error lies in that part of the program that carries out the different processing of record type A.

Obviously, the ideal is to achieve sharp distinctions between the IS and IS NOT sides of each part of the specification, but this is often not possible, and sometimes not necessary.

It is also obvious that if the distinctions are not very sharp then we cannot pinpoint likely areas so closely, and if there are no distinctions at all then the specification as it stands is not much good to us and it must be sharpened up, if possible, before proceeding.

9.3.3   Hypothesise about causes

When the specification is as good as possible, and distinctions can be seen between the IS and IS NOT sides of one or more parts of the specification, then we will have some pointers as to the area in which the error lies; one's experience can now be used to the full by hypothesising about possible causes of the deviation.

To use another canine analogy, the search for errors without any decent method of directing one's aim is rather like a bloodhound trying to pick up a robber's scent from among a number of different scents without any guidance as to which scent he should follow. In this situation the bloodhound will follow either the freshest or the nicest smell, and similarly the programmer might follow his nose along a path that proved profitable in a similar situation once before. But using The Method is like giving the bloodhound the robber's cap to sniff, after which he knows what he is looking for and can usually pick up and follow the correct scent quite easily.

9.3.4 Follow-up hypothesis

Having come up with a plausible theory, it will next be checked by examination of the program at that point, and hopefully a likely-looking error will be found there.

9.3.5 Verify suspected cause

Finally the erroneous part of the program can be dry run to make certain that the suspected error produces a deviation that *precisely* matches the specification. If it does, then the error has been found—positively. If the specification does not fit, then the cause found may be only part of the cause, or even no part of it at all, and in either case the answer is to try to improve the specification or the hypothesis.

In neither case does one say 'That looks like it, I'll try it and see.'

9.4 Examples of the use of The Method

We now illustrate the use of The Method by two simple examples, one a production problem, and one during poorly planned program testing. They have not been specially chosen, but are simply the first two examples that came to hand when this material was being developed. We use them precisely because they were chosen so randomly and because they would therefore seem to offer the reader the chance of seeing The Method in action in a real situation.

It is doubtful whether in such situations one would actually trouble to write down the specifications as they are here, but at least one would mentally write and analyse the specifications. With more difficult problems, however, where it is more important not to miss anything, and where clues are hard to find, it is a great help to write things down, as one can then pore over them in a much more concentrated fashion.

BROUGHT FORWARD	11/16	0.00	
MOVEMENTS	11/16	15.99	15.99
		- - - - - - - - - -	
BROUGHT FORWARD	11/123	19.01	
BROUGHT FORWARD	11/157	47.31	19.01
BROUGHT FORWARD	11/15	63.02	47.31
BROUGHT FORWARD	11/164	23.85	63.02
MOVEMENTS	11/164	23.86	47.71
		- - - - - - - - - -	
BROUGHT FORWARD	11/165	183.86	
BROUGHT FORWARD	11/173	0.00	183.86
MOVEMENTS	11/173	34.07	34.07
		- - - - - - - - - -	
BROUGHT FORWARD	11/17	8.03	
BROUGHT FORWARD	11/195	1.57	8.03
BROUGHT FORWARD	11/1	0.00	1.57
MOVEMENTS	11/1	16.90	16.90
		- - - - - - - - - -	
BROUGHT FORWARD	11/201	17.76	
BROUGHT FORWARD	11/205	145.95	17.76
MOVEMENTS	11/205	10.13	156.08
		- - - - - - - - - -	
BROUGHT FORWARD	11/206	34.98	
BROUGHT FORWARD	11/207	10.40	34.98
BROUGHT FORWARD	11/209	36.31	10.40
BROUGHT FORWARD	11/214	28.35	36.31
BROUGHT FORWARD	11/217	95.35	28.35
BROUGHT FORWARD	11/218	8.79	95.35
BROUGHT FORWARD	11/219	0.00	8.79
MOVEMENTS	11/219	42.24	42.24

Fig. 9.3 (a) The Method—Example 1—Schematic print layout

	Account No.	Brought Forward	Carried Forward
BROUGHT FORWARD	nn/nnn	999.99	
MOVEMENTS	nn/nnn	999.99	999.99
BROUGHT FORWARD	nn/nnn	999.99	
MOVEMENTS	nn/nnn	999.99	999.99

etc.

Movements

Fig. 9.3 (b) The Method—Example 1—Actual incorrect printout

9.4.1 Example 1

Program description

The program deals with the updating of a sales ledger and is in two parts. The first part updates the sales ledger file from a transactions tape, and for active accounts prints (amongst other things) b/f balance, movements, and c/f balance. The second part prints the same information in slightly different format, but for all accounts, active this month or not.

Deviation recognition

During a production run it was noticed that the second part of the program was printing wrongly. Figure 9.3(a) shows the schematic format expected and part of the actual printout is shown in Figure 9.3(b). Naturally there was no expected results schedule, but this was not too worrying, as the error would seem to be easy to find.

Deviation specification—1

Information was gathered from the printout and placed in the

78

appropriate category as shown in Figure 9.4, which is a first attempt at a specification of the deviation. Note the large amount of information that has been gathered and categorised.

Analysis for distinctions—1

WHAT   There is no distinction between the IS and IS NOT sides here, so the specification needs sharpening up. What is characteristic of the movements lines omitted (or printed)?

WHERE   An immediate distinction is apparent here: there is no fault in the printing of the movements during the first part of the program. Is there anything characteristic about the movements printed in the first part (or second part)?

WHEN   Again, a clear distinction is present, but it is not a very helpful one. The characteristic of production running is exhaustive testing, so this particular combination may not have been tested, or the deviation spotted during

?	IS	IS NOT
WHAT	Some movement lines and following underscoring not printed	1. _All_ movement lines and underscoring not printed. 2. Only movement lines missing. 3. Only underscoring missing
WHERE	Second part of printout	First part of printout
WHEN	During production run	Before live running
TO WHAT EXTENT	1. More movement lines ommitted than printed 2. Throughout second part of printout	1. More printed than omitted. 2. Patchy or transient fault

Fig. 9.4 The Method—Example 1—First error specification

program or system testing. Also there may have been an amendment since the program has been in production, and the amendment was not thoroughly tested, so the amendments list might possibly be checked.

EXTENT There is no real distinction here, but at least we are reassured that the fault seems consistent. It might be profitable to think a little about the fact that more movements are omitted than are printed; is there any clue there?

Deviation specification—2

Let us now see if we can sharpen up on the specification, and particularly to see if we can find out what is characteristic of the movements lines that are not printed.

By comparing the b/f and c/f totals we can find out the value of each movement line that is not printed. Figure 9.5 is a table of the values of the first few movements, whether or not they have been printed. It is clear from this table that the characteristic of omitted movement lines is that the value of the movement is zero.

We can now sharpen up the WHAT part of the specification to the extent that the IS side says that zero movements and the following underscoring are omitted, and the IS NOT side says that non-zero movements and the following underscoring are omitted. We must not forget that the omission of the underscoring each time must also be explained, but it seems so closely connected with the omission of the movement itself that the same error probably causes both deviations, so we can leave it for now, apart from bearing in mind that we must explain it in full.

Analysis for distinctions—2

There is now a clear distinction in the WHAT of the specification also, so we can move on to hypothesise about causes.

Hypothesise about causes

The cause now seems obvious—this is an error in the printing of zero movements, a conclusion supported by the following points:

(a) The error does not occur while printing is taking place during the first part of the program; but active accounts, by definition, have non-zero movements, so the first part of the program never attempts to print any zero movements lines.

(b) More movement lines are omitted than printed, and a general characteristic of this business may be that each month there are more inactive customers than active ones.

Look for bug

The first thing to do is to look through the amendments since production running began, but none of the amendments appear relevant.

Upon examination of the program a paragraph called PRINT-ZERO-MOVES is noticed, which obviously looks promising, and in fact, it is found that the zero movement line is set up but is never actually printed.

Value	Omitted	Printed
15.99		✓
0.00	✓	
0.00	✓	
0.00	✓	
23.86		✓
0.00	✓	
34.07		✓
0.00	✓	
0.00	✓	
16.90		✓
0.00	✓	
10.13		✓
0.00	✓	
0.00	✓	
0.00	✓	
0.00	✓	
0.00	✓	
0.00	✓	
42.24		✓

Fig. 9.5 The Method—Example 1—Values of movements omitted

Verification of suspected cause

Dry running of this part of the program readily reveals that the error found reproduces the whole of the specified deviation, including the omission of the underscoring. In fact, there are two errors, one of them being the omission of the writing of the movements line, and the other the omission of a separate write to do the underscoring.

Bug elimination

There are no problems here, two PERFORMS only being required. But the amendments must be thoroughly checked before submission of the program for a test of the amendments.

Summary

This may seem an awfully long-winded way to solve a simple problem, and the reader may feel that a complicated problem would be hopelessly difficult to solve in this way. But in fact the reverse is the case.

What the example should have illustrated is how much information is available if one looks for it; if one knows how to classify and represent it well; and if one has a way of looking for further information. How many people, for example, would have assumed that the underscoring would return by correcting the 'obvious' error, and how many would never have spotted that the underscoring was missing in the first place?

It is easy to concentrate on only one aspect of a deviation, but the specification forces one to consider all aspects, and in addition, of course, the specification positively encourages the dry running of the suspected cause, and of the correction, thus avoiding the correction of only half the error.

9.4.2 Example 2

Program description

This program reads a product file until a live product header record is found, and a list of depots stocking this product is then prepared by reference to a table read in from magnetic tape.

	EXPECTED			ACTUAL	
PROD CODE	DEPOT	RECORD TYPE	PROD CODE	DEPOT	RECORD TYPE
0009	01	PRODUCT HEADER	0009		PRODUCT HEADER
0009	02	DEPOT STOCK RECORD	0009	GH	DEPOT STOCK RECORD
0009	03	DEPOT STOCK RECORD	0009		DEPOT STOCK RECORD
0009	04	DEPOT STOCK RECORD	0009	SH	DEPOT STOCK RECORD
0009	05	DEPOT STOCK RECORD	0009	W	DEPOT STOCK RECORD
0009	06	DEPOT STOCK RECORD	0009	L	DEPOT STOCK RECORD
0009	07	DEPOT STOCK RECORD	0009		DEPOT STOCK RECORD
0009	08	DEPOT STOCK RECORD	0010		PRODUCT HEADER
0010	01	PRODUCT HEADER	0010	GH	DEPOT STOCK RECORD
0010	02	DEPOT STOCK RECORD	0010		DEPOT STOCK RECORD
0010	03	DEPOT STOCK RECORD	0010	SH	DEPOT STOCK RECORD
0010	04	DEPOT STOCK RECORD	0010	W	DEPOT STOCK RECORD
0010	05	DEPOT STOCK RECORD	0010	L	DEPOT STOCK RECORD
0010	06	DEPOT STOCK RECORD	0010		DEPOT STOCK RECORD
0010	07	DEPOT STOCK RECORD			
0010	08	DEPOT STOCK RECORD			

Fig. 9.6 The Method—Example 2—Incorrect printout

Deviation recognition

In this particular example each item is stocked by depots 01 to 08, and the expected printout for two such depots is shown in Figure 9.6, together with the actual test printout.

Deviation specification

Information was gathered from the printout and placed in the appropriate category as shown in Figure 9.7, which is a first attempt at a specification of the deviation. Our first thought from the specification is that it is likely that we are looking for two errors, rather than one, one error being connected with the missing line, and the other with the depot code.

Analysis for distinctions

WHAT   The only distinction between the IS and the IS NOT sides is that all depot codes are wrong and not just some of them, and that they follow a consistent pattern.

We should like to be able to get closer than this; to be able to say, for instance, which line is omitted, so as to find out whether or not it is always the same one and also to discover what is characteristic of this line.

?	IS	IS NOT
WHAT	1. All depot codes wrong: some blank, some alphabetic: consistent pattern. 2. One line missing for each product header.	1. Some codes wrong, some numeric but wrong: random pattern. 2. More than one line missing
WHERE	Rubbish in depot code column of printout	Any other column
WHEN	On first test	On any other test
TO WHAT EXTENT	Throughout printout for every product printed.	Patchy or transient

Fig. 9.7 The Method—Example 2—First error specification

WHERE   There is no distinction here, except that the depot code is the only field with rubbish in it, which suggests that the error is confined to the processing of this field alone.

WHEN   Again there is no distinction here: this is the first test, so there are no previous test results to refer to. Had there been a previous test, it would have been possible for something to have been altered by accident when amending the program after the test.

EXTENT   Yet again we have no distinction, simply reassurance that it is not a random error.

It is plain that the specification is not sharp enough, and we should particularly like to know which line is missing, but the only way in which we can identify lines is by depot code: and the depot code is rubbish!

At this stage we have to admit that the specification cannot be sharpened up, so we simply feel that we have two errors, one to do with the missing line, and one connected with the rubbishy depot code. The depot code error seems slightly easier to deal with, so let us look for that one first.

Hypothesise about causes

The consistent rubbish suggests that the program is picking up the wrong field, or that there is a conversion error, or both.

Look for errors—depot code

Since depot code is picked up from the table read in from magnetic tape, it is sensible to check the table layout, and while doing this it is found that the program has described the table incorrectly. In fact the depot code position referred to two characters of an alphabetic field, and these two characters were those printed out, except that the characters for depot 01 were missing.

Look for errors—missing line

It is now entirely reasonable to suppose that the missing line is caused by incorrect depot 01 processing. The logic of the table-processing part of the program is shown in Figure 9.8, from which it can readily be seen that the details of the first depot are being read, but are not being stored for printing, so that line gets missed.

85

Verify suspected causes

Once again, dry running of the program as it stands reproduces the precise deviation specified.

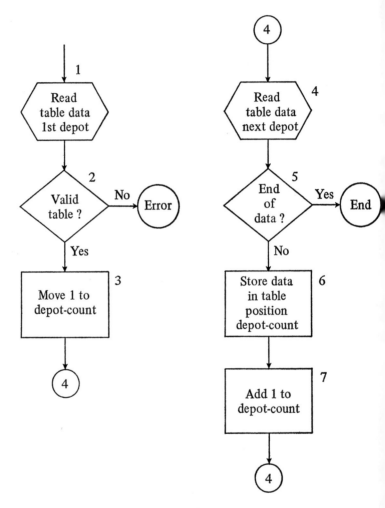

Fig. 9.8 The Method—Example 2—Logic in error

Bug elimination

A little more difficult this time, but still trivial, really; simply altering the table layout and the flow of the table processing. We must remember to dry-run the amendments.

Summary

In this case the specification was by no means precise, but it did at least indicate that there were two errors, and it told us that information as to which line was missing would help us quite a lot. Fortunately the depot code error was easily found, and dry-running it also shed a lot of light on the second error. This gradual unveiling is typical of a multi-error situation, where one uses information gained from one error to help solve another.

D

10 Debugging case study –
Program design and writing

In this and the following chapter we prove our point by taking the reader through every stage in the writing and testing of a program, hiding nothing as we go. At every stage of this work we have tried to practise all that we have been preaching so far. We believe that there can be no sterner test of our methods than to demonstrate them in a live and realistic situation, and we confidently leave you to judge the results.

10.1 The program

10.1.1 Program specification

The program specification (with the omission of the print layout, which is self-evident from the printout shown later) is given in Appendix 1. It can be seen that the program validates input card transactions to a stock update run. Valid cards are written to magnetic tape, invalid cards are printed, and control totals are accumulated and printed.

The validation to be done is shown in Figure 10.1.

The program as specified would be fairly realistic for a simple stock recording system, and has the advantage that it is straightforward enough for the reader to be able to grasp the processing required, but complex enough for the program to be badly designed.

10.1.2 Language used

Cobol was the obvious choice, because most programmers can at least understand a Cobol program, even though they may not be able to write one. But in addition to this, it was chosen because Cobol is a language that is often very badly used, and we wished to show

Field	Valid contents
Transaction code	15, 20, 25, 30, 35 or 45
Stock no.	All numeric — valid check digit greater than zero — no leading spaces
Quantity	All numeric — greater than zero — leading spaces allowed
Customer no. Supplier no.	As stock no.
Credit note and despatch note numbers	First character alphabetic — next six numeric — no spaces
Date	Format DDMMYY — valid date (inc. leap year) — year 70 to 89 inc. Leading space allowed in day and month
Unused columns	Blanks

Fig. 10.1 Case study program—Field validation

something of how it could be used much better.

The Cobol facilities used would be available on most compilers, with the exception of the COMPUTE verb, which we used for a reason that will be explained later.

0.1.3 Computer used

We had a choice here between ICL 1900 and IBM 360. In point of fact, the machine has relatively little effect upon the programming, and we eventually chose the 360 under DOS because:

    (a) The operating system monitors the running of the program more closely, giving greater chance of program 'checks' (i.e. failures).

    (b) We felt that, in general, we might get more interesting errors than on the 1900.

    (c) Job control adds an extra hurdle.

10.2 The programmers

10.2.1 Number of programmers

Even though the program was written and tested monolithically, two programmers were used full time on it, one of them being Arnold Sampson and the other Neal Stockwell. The reasons for using two programmers were:

   (a) Two heads are better than one in an exercise like this.

   (b) There was a fairly severe time constraint upon the work, only two or three weeks being available.

   (c) Arnold Sampson did not at that time have any 360 programming experience.

10.2.2 Age and experience

At the time of writing the program both programmers were aged 28–30, and both had had 6–7 years' experience. Their experience had differed widely: Stockwell's had been mainly scientific, and on the 360 under OS, with little Cobol or DOS experience; while Sampson's had been mainly commercial, was completely non-360, and had not touched Cobol since he lectured on 1900 Cobol three years earlier.

10.2.3 Split of work

Sampson designed the program, including how to use debugging aids, designed the first test pack, coded about a third of the Procedure Division, and checked Stockwell's coding. Stockwell designed the second test pack, did the rest of the coding, and checked Sampson's coding.

Both programmers did the test plan, the dry running, the testing, and the amending together.

10.3 Program design

This section will go through the various design points in the order in which they were discussed in earlier chapters, and aims to put flesh on those bones.

0.3.1 Program structure

The program is monolithic in the sense that it can only be compiled and tested as a whole, but it is modular in the sense that it is divided into sections and has lower routines that:

(a) have a functional identity;
(b) whose logic is relatively simple, and so easily testable;
(c) whose input and output is simple.

Figure 10.2 shows the overall structure and gives further detail of the validation section, which illustrates the modular–monolithic structure best. It can be deduced from the diagram that each 'module'

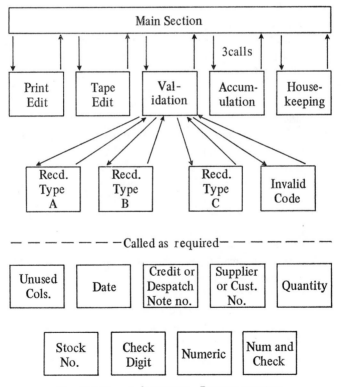

Fig. 10.2 Case study program—Program structure

consists largely of calls to lower level modules, and this hierarchical structure is typical of modular programs. The effects of this structure on ease of amendments, for instance, are described below.

10.3.2 Programming for errors

The main point to emphasise here is that, as this is a validation program, no assumptions at all must be made about the input: the program must happily cope with blank cards, object decks, and even the proverbial sliced loaf! Robustness is mandatory.

10.3.3 Programming for amendments

Modular design

When making any program amendment one wants to be able to identify fairly easily the part of the program that needs amending, but, probably more important, one would like to know the chances of an alteration in this part of the program causing a change in another, completely unrelated, part. This is often known as the 'plate of spaghetti' situation: pull it here and something moves on the other side.

The functional identity of modules helps very significantly in the area of finding out which part of the program must be altered. For instance, the introduction of a range check upon one or more fields in an adjustments card would be easily tied down to an amendment to the routine called VALIDATE-ADJUSTS.

The 'spaghetti effect' is usually caused by programmers taking advantage of convenient situations. Such practices are generally the result of laziness, lack of awareness of their dangers, or a search for extra 'efficiency', although most programmers would only ever give the final reason if asked why they do it. There are occasions where the saving of core is vital, and there are other occasions where the saving of microseconds is important, but in most programming environments the most pressing need is to have simple, well-designed programs that can be amended quickly, easily and, above all, safely. In these cases spaghetti programming is inexcusable.

The aim of the case study program in this area has therefore been to make no false savings and to keep interfaces between routines

'clean' by having routines connected only by their obvious parameters like data fields and error flags. Thus no advantage has been
taken of the fact that all input record types have a stock number and
a quantity punched in the same positions, because otherwise the
introduction of a new format for a record would mean that for this
record type the program would have to branch to a special routine,
and this could easily snowball.

A similar situation would arise in a spaghetti program if a new
record type altogether were introduced, but with the design used
a new record type would basically involve an extra test to recognise
it, and a routine to validate this record type. It would also require
an amendment to the routine that validates input transactions whose
code the program cannot recognise, because this routine currently
does its helpful best to validate the contents of the record, which
involves assuming the consistency of the position of these fields.
Deletion of record types is equally simple.

Programming standards

From the point of view of easy program amendment the relevant
standards are those concerned with coding and documentation, and
details of the standards used are given below. No particular set
of standards has been used but a fictitious (hopefully) set has been
followed.

Coding standards

The main points here are that the coding has been kept very simple
and straightforward; data and procedure names have been made
reasonably long and meaningful; and the coding has been well laid
out, with indentation and blank lines being used a lot.

Of lesser importance are the way in which sequence numbering
has been used (with gaps being left between sequence numbers and
with blocks of numbers allocated to different sections), the in-
crementing of level numbers by two, and the use of condition names
to give more explicit coding.

Appendix 2 shows a few sample pages of program listing to
illustrate these points.

Documentation standards

Throughout the program itself comments were inserted frequently and at standard places—at the front of each module or section, and wherever else the programmer felt that a comment would help. Comments are very important because they are part of the source listing, which is quite often the only up-to-date documentation of a program.

Other forms of documentation used were the specification (Appendix 1), a macro flowchart (Appendix 3), an automatically drawn detailed flowchart (part of which is given as Appendix 4) and a cross-reference listing (partially shown in Appendix 5). Thus the amending programmer can steadily work down in level of understanding, so as to find out where the program must be altered, and he has the detailed flowchart and cross-reference listing to enable him to make the amendments quickly and completely.

10.3.4 Use of debugging aids

Analysis of program complexity – Logical complexity

Validation programs usually contain a certain amount of logical complexity, and this one is no exception, but the complexity is minimised by the modular design used. Only one routine—the one used to validate dates—contains anything more than trivial logic, so generally all that needs to be verified is:

The correct calling of routines.
The correct passing of input parameters.
The correct operation of the routine, meaning the correctness of the output from the routine.

File complexity

There is no file complexity, which again is typical of validation programs.

Arithmetic complexity

The only suggestion of arithmetic complexity here is in the validation of the check digits, so some monitoring of the calculation will be required, more to show how to do it than because it is strictly necessary.

Use of aids – Aids used

It will surprise nobody who has read Chapter 6 to learn that it was felt that using DISPLAY as a snapshot print could cope with the monitoring requirements outlined above, meaning that we will be using a snapshot as both a snapshot and a trace.

Positioning and use of aids

An analysis of the detailed program structure shows that in only ten of the routines was there any real justification for using debug prints to monitor their performance. These routines and the way in which the aids were used within them are as follows:

(a) Main section
   Here the snapshots were used to:
   Print the state of the debug switches (q.v.) after input.
   Print the transaction code after reading a card, because the transaction code controls the validation part of the program flow.
   Print the state of the error flags upon return from the validation section, as the state of these flags controls the writing part of the program flow.

(b) VALIDATE-STOCK-NO, VALIDATE-QUANTITY, VALIDATE-SUPP-OR-CUST-NO, VALIDATE-CREDIT-OR-DESP-NO, VALIDATE-NUM-AND-CHECK, VALIDATE-NUMERIC.
   In these routines the snapshots were used to print, just after entry and just before the exit, the contents of the fields to be validated and the state of the error flags, thus checking the action of the routine concerned.

(c) VALIDATE-DATE
   The monitoring for this routine is as for (b) above, but with an intermediate print to establish whether or not the correct month ending day has been picked up.

(d) VALIDATE-CHECK-DIGIT
   Once again the input and output is printed as in (b) above, but

95

in addition to this the arithmetical operation is checked at two intermediate stages of the calculation: by printing out the weighted sum of the digits; and by printing out the initial check digit, i.e. the remainder from the calculation before changing 10 into zero.

Conditioning the print

The printing of the snapshots for each of the ten routines is controlled by a separate switch, so that ten debugging switches are required.

Print format

The format of each snapshot print is

	Identification	Parameter Details
	nn/nnnnnn	xxxx---xxx
Controlling switch no.	Sequence no. of line in program.	

10.4 Pre-test planning

10.4.1 The Test Plan

The test plan was prepared after the initial program design, and is given as Appendix 6. The main points of the plan are as follows:

Three test packs were required—a simple one, a complex one, and an object deck. The first test pack was intended to be used for dry running, and then to verify most of the program quickly, thus allowing debug prints to be turned off when the other test packs were used.

It was clear even at this stage which debugging aids should be utilised and the way in which they should be used.

The expected results had to be left until later because the test data had not yet been designed.

10.4.2 Design of test data

The test data was designed immediately before coding began, and this turned out to be a very useful exercise, because on several occasions the thought that went into the design of the data, and the questions that were asked, revealed gaps in the logic of the program. One hesitates to suggest that test data should always be designed at this stage, because the time during which the program is punched is such a convenient time to design data, but if it is possible to choose, then do the design before the coding and you might also find some flaws in your logic thereby.

The functions of the first test pack have already been mentioned, and the only routine that it does not completely verify is VALIDATE-DATE, so the second test pack gives the date routine a hammering, as well as adding volume problems and a blank card. The third test pack, the object deck, is the final test of robustness.

0.4.3 Expected results

Expected results schedules were actually done, and are shown as Appendix 7. The first one is really the schematic from which the first test pack was compiled, the schematic having been produced as described in Chapter 7, while the second one is a normal sort of expected results schedule. Neither is very brilliant, but they were both adequate in their respective ways.

10.5 Program development log

Both programmers kept a detailed log of their work, but only one of them is reproduced here (as Appendix 8) and the level of detail given should be noted.

10.6 Desk checking

Each programmer checked both his own and the other man's work, and some spelling mistakes and missing periods were found. But, being human, some errors were also missed.

10.7 Dry running

97

10.7.1 Data used

The first test pack was used and was completely dry run.

10.7.2 Errors found

The following errors were found and corrected:
  (a) Totals not initialised.
  (b) INTERMEDIATE too small.
  (c) Illegal IF statement.
  (d) Illegal MULTIPLY statement.
  (e) The logic of the EXAMINE statement in the date checking routine was wrong.
  (f) Illegal MOVE statement.
  (g) Wrong spelling of a data name.

The compiler would not have found all of these errors, since some of them are logic errors rather than syntax ones, so the dry running exercise was deemed useful in this case.

10.7.3 Improvement of efficiency

During the dry running it was discovered that usage COMPUTA-TIONAL (i.e. binary) had often been used in preference to COM-PUTATIONAL-3 (i.e. packed decimal), where in fact COM-PUTATIONAL-3 would have been the better usage. This situation had arisen because of Stockwell's scientific background—where pure binary is naturally used—and Sampson's ICL1900 background—where COMPUTATIONAL is the best usage for fields on which arithmetic is to be performed.

It was decided to correct this situation by changing the usages in a number of cases, and we were human enough not to check out thoroughly the effects of these later changes. The effects of this lack of thoroughness will become apparent in the next chapter.

This illustrates the truism that it is better to design and code the program properly in the first place than to amend it later, which again pushes the emphasis back to the planning/design stage, instead of the testing stage.

At this point the program was ready for punching and testing, and the next chapter describes what happened.

11 Debugging case study—Program testing

In this chapter we continue the case study by examining the testing in detail, but we should first point out that we are mainly concerned with finding errors and their causes. The correction of the errors found, though obviously important in the overall testing context, is not of much interest to us here. All that we really need to say about error correction is that it must be carried out with at least as much thought, care, and thoroughness as the original program writing, and also that the correction must be dry run to ensure that the whole of the specified deviation is removed by it.

11.1 Card listing and checking

If it is convenient to do so, it is a wise precaution to have the program, job control, and test packs listed and checked because one or more compilations and/or tests can be saved thereby. In this case it was convenient, and so the program, the job control, and the first and second test packs were duly listed and checked, with the result that several punching errors were found and corrected.

11.2 Compilation

On the first compilation there were a number of E (error) messages, which prevented the attempted test from executing, as well as a number of W (warning) messages also. Most of the messages related to the usual errors like missing periods, wrongly spelt datanames, and missing quotes in literals, but three errors were particularly annoying:
  (a) Wrong format of a MULTIPLY statement, i.e.
     MULTIPLY INTERMEDIATE BY 11 (trying to put the

result in the literal) instead of
MULTIPLY 11 BY INTERMEDIATE.
(b) DIVIDE RESULT BY 11 GIVING INTERMEDIATE
(which some compilers would now accept) instead of
DIVIDE 11 INTO RESULT GIVING INTERMEDIATE.
(c) The VALUE clauses used to zeroise the totals were illegal
because the totals fields were sub-fields of a field described
using OCCURS.

The first two errors would not have been perpetrated had the
programmers' Cobol knowledge been better, but they should have
been spotted during desk checking. The third error was the result of a
faulty correction to one of the errors found during dry running, and
it illustrates how easy it is to 'correct' something wrongly. Once again
the third error was due to a lack of Cobol expertise, but it was still
pretty inexcusable. After correction of the E errors and those W
errors that were significant (in IBM Cobol many W errors are
rarely corrected), it was felt that the next compilation would be good
enough to allow execution of the first test.

11.3 First test

11.3.1 Test pack and diagnostic switches

The first test pack was used and all ten diagnostic switches were
turned on.

11.3.2 Results

Only 24 W errors were detected on the second compilation, and so
link-editing and execution took place, terminated by a program check
on a data exception, with a consequent dump.

A printout was produced (Appendix 9) containing some debug
prints but no error records, and no records were written to the file of
valid transactions. In other words, if no debug prints had been
included then there would have been no printed output at all. Thus
the test would only have found one error—the one causing the data
exception.

11.3.3 Checking the results

Before looking at the message about the data exception, the program was dry run with the first card of the test pack to check the course and actions of the program. It was immediately noticed that the debug prints were not printing precisely as expected: blanks, parentheses, and asterisks appeared where zeros or ones were expected, and as the contents of these prints were important some tentative conclusions about the meanings of these characters had to be drawn.

The first debug print that looked strange was print 10/600090, which is printed upon entry to the accumulation section. The print shows the totals of records read, written, or rejected in each of the categories, depending upon the value in CONTROL-TYPE. In this case the totals had just been zeroised in the housekeeping section, and CONTROL-TYPE contained 1, asking for an accumulation and print of records read. This print contained *bb)* for each of the totals, instead of the 00000 that we expected, so we could immediately suspect that a packed field of five digits was being printed as a character field of three bytes, with the consequent difficulty of interpreting packed bytes as characters. But regardless of the reason, it looked as though we could treat a *)* in such a debug print as zero.

This conclusion tended to be confirmed by the next print, 10/600280, which is printed before exit from the accumulation section, and which prints the same totals as on input to the section. In this case the section should have added 1 to the first (transaction code 15) and last (total records read) totals, and we see that these two figures have changed from *bb)* to *bb**, implying that we can treat *** here as *1*. (So, in the New Maths, *)+1=*!*).

Similarly, the debug prints showing the contents of validation flags showed a *)* instead of the expected zero, so the same assumption would appear to apply here also.

On the basis of this assumption the debug prints that were printed showed, by their order and contents, that the card had been properly recognised and validated which was a lot more than no debug prints could have shown.

The final debug print showed that no error flags had been set, i.e. that it was a valid transaction, so the program should have gone to PROCESS-VALID-TRANS, the first two statements of which are

101

MOVE 2 TO CONTROL-TYPE.
PERFORM ACCUMULATION.

The first statement in the accumulation section is a debug print, but this never appeared, so it looked as though the program-stopping error must have occurred shortly after return from the validation section.

It therefore seemed as though there were two errors to investigate and cure:

(a) the data exception;
(b) the mis-printing of the debug prints.

11.3.4 Error 1–data exception

Suspected instruction

From the point (sequence no. 400300) where the final debug print was produced to the point where the next debug print should have been produced there were only three statements that could have caused a data exception:

(a) The IF statement (sequence no. 400330) that examines the main error flag to decide whether or not to treat the record as a valid transaction.

(b) If the main error flag was zero, as thought, and if the IF statement worked correctly, the program should have gone to PROCESS-VALID-TRANS (sequence no. 400550), and the first statement, MOVE 2 to CONTROL-TYPE, could have been the culprit.

(c) Similarly, if the IF statement had gone the other way to that expected, the program would have gone to PROCESS-INVALID-TRANS (sequence no. 400740), and the first statement here, MOVE 3 to CONTROL-TYPE, could equally well have been responsible.

However, after reading this card in, the program had successfully executed statement 400260, MOVE 1 TO CONTROL-TYPE, so moving 2 or 3 to this field should be equally valid. This identifies the IF as the culprit.

Now, and only now, was the data exception message examined, and the address it gave was the address of the IF, so the conclusion was confirmed.

(We did not then realise that the address of a data exception is always an address in the program, so we wanted to see if we could pinpoint the faulty instruction without back-tracking from an address in some software routine. Had we realised this, then we should have looked directly at the message, but only after checking all of the results first, as already described. Nevertheless, it was an interesting exercise, and it shows how the careful positioning of the debug prints narrowed the search to only three possible statements.)

Suspected cause

The IF compared, via a condition name, the contents of MAIN-FLAG, a signed COMPUTATIONAL-3 field, with a literal of 0, so the only possibility of a data error was that the contents of MAIN-FLAG were not COMPUTATIONAL-3.

In fact, LOW-VALUES (binary zeros) had been moved to VALIDATION-FLAGS, a group field containing MAIN-FLAG, and since group fields are regarded as being ALPHANUMERIC, MAIN-FLAG therefore received a binary zero (X'00') instead of a COMPUTATIONAL-3 signed zero (X'0C' or X'0F').

Thus the contents and usage of the field became incompatible.

Verification of cause

The deviation caused by this error is very simple, and is specified in

?	IS	IS NOT
WHAT	Data exception	Any other exception
WHERE	IF TRANSACTION-IS-VALID	Any other statement encountered so far
WHEN	First test - first time statement encountered	Second or subsequent time
EXTENT	—	—

Fig. 11.1 Case study program—Data exception error specification

Figure 11.1. It is plain from this specification that the invalid contents of MAIN-FLAG will cause the deviation as specified.

Correction

There is no real reason why the flags should not be ALPHA-NUMERIC fields, so their usage, pictures and condition names were changed accordingly. But this on its own would not have been enough, because the move of LOW-VALUES would still have put binary zeros into MAIN-FLAG, so the statement was changed to a move of ZEROES.

Comments

This was a rather untidy error that does not reflect much credit on the authors. Originally the fields concerned were described as COMPUTATIONAL, hence the move of LOW-VALUES, but their usage was changed to COMPUTATIONAL-3 as part of the 'improvement' of efficiency. At that time, instead of just changing all COMPUTATIONAL fields to COMPUTATIONAL-3, which was mostly what happened, the whole question of the usage of the fields concerned should have been examined and this would have led to a decision to go ALPHANUMERIC. But even accepting the change to COMPUTATIONAL-3, this change was not carried out thoroughly, because:

    (a) the pictures of the flags were left at S9, the S having been required for COMPUTATIONAL, instead of being changed to simply 9;

    (b) the invalid zeroising of the fields was not spotted and changed.

11.3.5 Error 2–wrong printing of debug prints

In order to interpret the contents of those debug prints showing totals and the settings of flags, it had been tentatively concluded that b or $)$ represented a zero and * represented a 1. The reason for the misprinting had even been suggested; that an attempt was being made to interpret as characters the contents of these COMPUTATIONAL-3 fields. But now these theories had to be examined thoroughly.

Field contents – Totals

As explained above, the totals had all been individually zeroised in the housekeeping section by having ZERO moved to them, so they would then each contain a valid COMPUTATIONAL-3 zero. Then two of the totals had had a literal of 1 added to them, and these two (the first and the last printed) would then contain a valid COMPUTATIONAL-3 one.

Flags

We have already seen that the initial zeroising of the validation flags was done wrongly, and that it left each flag with binary zeros in it, which are invalid in a COMPUTATIONAL-3 field. During the course of the program three flags which are used as error flags for very low level routines, had had ZERO moved individually to them, and this had therefore filled them with a valid COMPUTATIONAL-3 zero.

Suspected cause

Given this information about the field contents and our suspicions about trying to interpret packed bytes as characters, we could only suspect that the fields were being printed in an incorrect fashion. Upon examining the statements concerned, it was found that in every case either TOTALS-PART or VALIDATION-FLAGS, both of them group-fields, was being DISPLAYed. Therefore, since DISPLAY treats a group-field as ALPHANUMERIC, the program was, as we thought, attempting to interpret the packed bytes as characters, and had failed. This was supported by the fact that in another debug print, 9/703690, the contents of the COMPUTATIONAL-3 fields MULTIPLIER and COUNT, when DISPLAYed individually, had been printed correctly as 7 and 000 respectively.

Verification of cause

The specification of the deviation is given in Figure 11.2 and it can be seen that the DISPLAYing of the group fields containing the contents already described will give the results described therein. Notice that the explanation must explain the different printing of the last three validation flags.

105

?	IS	IS NOT
WHAT	1. Printing of bb) for 0 and bb * for 1 in TOTALS-PART 2. Printing of) or b for 0 in VALIDATION-FLAGS	Printing of correct or any other character for 0 and 1
WHERE	1. TOTALS-PART 2. VALIDATION-FLAGS	1. MULTIPLIER for 7 2. COUNT for 1
WHEN	When displaying these fields for printing. On first test.	During any other printing. (none done)
EXTENT	Every time displayed 1. TOTALS-PART whenever it contains 0's or 1's 2. VALIDATION-FLAGS: get b except when individual flag has just had zero moved into it.	A random error. The other way round.

Fig. 11.2 Case study program—Wrong printing specification

Correction

The totals were DISPLAYed individually, but the printing of th
validation flags was left as it was because of the change of thei
usage from COMPUTATIONAL-3 to ALPHANUMERIC.

Comments

The lesson here is that the production of debug prints involve
programming, and therefore the coding involved must be checke
just as rigorously as any other part of the program. Clearly th
authors were guilty of a certain thoughtlessness where they shoul
have taken more care, because one cannot easily debug the pro
gram from faulty debug prints.

In a sense one could say that there was only a single error foun
because both errors described display a common fault: usin
group fields in cases where the elementary sub-fields should hav

been used. This quite basic but very common fault should not have occurred, and should have been detected during desk-checking or dry running. But then if the authors had been perfect, the testing of the program would have been a useless exercise as far as this book is concerned!

11.4 Second test

11.4.1 Test pack and diagnostic switches

The first test pack was used, and all ten diagnostic switches were turned on, because none of the program had yet been thoroughly validated.

11.4.2 Results

The compilation again showed only W errors, so link-editing and execution took place. The program went right through to the end of the test pack, printed debug prints, error reports, and control totals, and wrote a number of records to the disc, which was subsequently printed via a utility. Part of the printout produced is shown in Appendix 10.

11.4.3 Checking the results

Because the program had done so much, the error reports, control totals and disc print were checked first. Everything was found to be in order, so there was no need to check the debug prints.

11.4.4 Comments

To go right through the first test pack correctly on the second test is not too bad at all, so this time it seems as though the authors deserve a pat on the back—for a change.

11.5 Third test

11.5.1 Test pack and diagnostic switches

The first test pack had now served its purpose, and so the second

107

test pack was used. It will be remembered that the main purpose of the second test pack was to validate the date routine thoroughly, and therefore its diagnostic switch (6) and the main section's switch (1) were left on.

11.5.2 Results

The program went right through to the end of the second test pack, printed debug prints, error reports, and control totals, and wrote a number of records to the disc, which again was subsequently printed back via a utility. Part of the printout is shown as Appendix 11.

11.5.3 Checking the results

Again the debug prints were ignored for the present, the error reports, control totals, and disc print being checked first. This time one error was found: a record with the invalid date 29.02.71 was found to be valid.

11.5.4 Date error

Suspected cause

The date concerned was included specifically to check the operation of the leap year calculation, and since 1971 was not a leap year, the date should have been found invalid. The leap year calculation used the COMPUTE verb, as follows:

COMPUTE LY-TEST-FIELD = COMP-YEAR – (COMP-YEAR/4*4).

The logic is that if COMP-YEAR is exactly divisible by 4 then LY-TEST-FIELD will end up containing zero, and this would indicate that the year involved is a leap year. The method obviously requires that the intermediate result of the calculation (i.e. COMP-YEAR/4) should be integral only, because if it contained any decimal places the following situation might arise:

$$\frac{COMP\text{-}YEAR\,(71)}{4} = 17.75$$

$17.75 \times 4 = 71 = COMP\text{-}YEAR$

Therefore 71 is a leap year.

In fact, when Stockwell coded the COMPUTE, he said that he suspected that the intermediate result might contain decimals, so that the above situation would arise. The statement was, however, left as it was, largely to see just what would happen.

The debug prints for the record (6/702390, 6/702670 & 6/702970) should have thrown some light on the matter, but in fact they only showed that the date had got into the validation area correctly, that MAX-DAYS was 28 (as it should be) and that DATE-FLAG had not been set. In other words no information was given about the result of the leap year calculation. Considering that the calculation was thought to be suspect, then if it was not to be altered, at least it should have been monitored by a debug print. But in fact there is no way in which a debug print can help, because one cannot get at the intermediate result, which is the one that holds the key.

Verification of cause

The specification of the deviation is given in Figure 11.3, and one can see from it that the incorrect validation of the date would cause the deviation given, and the circumstantial evidence given above would seem to be sufficient to prove that it is the non-truncation of the intermediate result that is at fault. But in fact, since there was a dump available from the first test, it was examined to see what the COMPUTE was doing. This examination showed that four byte arithmetic was used, i.e. that decimals were being kept.

?	IS	IS NOT
WHAT	Invalid date of 29·02·71 found valid	Any other date fault
WHERE	2nd. test pack	1st. & 2nd. test pack
WHEN	3rd. test when date is 29·02·71	1st. or 2nd. test Any other date
EXTENT	Once only	More than once

Fig. 11.3 Case study program—Date error specification

109

Correction

The correction chosen was to break the calculation into three separate arithmetic operations, thus controlling the intermediate field.

Comments

This error demonstrates the danger of powerful verbs like COMPUTE, which work in hidden ways. Really, it should not have been used, but it was left in for interest's sake, which is perhaps not the best reason for using a particular verb or technique.

It is interesting to see that no debug print could confirm the working of the COMPUTE, and one could perhaps learn a lesson from this: do not use statements when you cannot, even if you don't want to, monitor their operation closely.

11.6 Fourth test

11.6.1 Test pack and diagnostic switches

This was expected to be the final test, since the only remaining error on the first and second test packs was the date error. So the first and second test packs were used, together with an object deck, and all diagnostic switches were turned off.

11.6.2 Results

The program went right through all test packs to the end, printed error reports and control totals, and wrote a number of records to the disc, which again was subsequently printed back.

11.6.3 Checking the results

There were no debug prints to check, but the date error was checked to ensure that it had been cured, and the other printout was checked carefully, too. No error was found, so the program could be pronounced bug-free.

11.7 Conclusions

This program, of about 20K bytes, was written and tested by two programmers, neither of whom was an expert on the machine/ language combination used, in about five man weeks, using about 45 minutes 360/30 CPU time, with four tests and one previous compilation. Whether the reader regards this as being good or not we do not really know, but we would consider the number of tests and the amount of machine time used to be below average, and the amount of man time used to be above average. Probably 3–4 weeks would be a reasonable allocation for the program, but the time used here was pretty well bound to be excessive in the circumstances, given that the program was being written as an example of good practice, and that there would be no opportunity for covering up any errors made. Let's face it, very few people would be willing to have their work in such circumstances held up for all to see, and those who would might expect a little longer than usual.

On the credit side, the effort taken before reaching the machine seemed to pay off. Four tests, using three test packs, with only three errors found, one of which was suspected beforehand, and one of which was connected with the debug prints themselves, can only be called a first class result, and would appear to prove the bug avoidance part of the ideas set out in this book.

As far as recognising and eliminating bugs is concerned, we had explained before that The Method would only play a supporting role, and so it turned out. In fact, for only one of the errors (wrong printing of debug prints) was there any real justification for using The Method at all. But do not forget The Method: when things get difficult, and mental contortions will not do, it comes into its own.

We are left only with the use of the debug prints, and their usefulness was shown very well on the first test, when they enabled a lot of information to be extracted from what, to most programmers, would have been a fairly unproductive test. Also, going through debug prints somehow gives one greater confidence in the program than straightforward examination of test printout ever can. On the other tests the prints were not really required because of the lack of errors, but they were there, ready to yield the back-up information to the bare printed fact if required.

Have we, therefore, proved the bug elimination part of our method? We would suspect that the bug avoidance was so good that we have not quite made our case fully for the bug elimination, but we are not willing to fiddle the answers until we do. Yet we can assure the

111

reader that the bug elimination methods are as powerful and as effective as the bug avoidance ones, and we would simply suggest that you try them to see if they work for you as they do for us.

Part IV In a modular environment

12 Modular programming

So far this book has confined itself to talking about techniques that are useful whether or not a modular programming scheme is in operation. Now we want to talk specifically about testing in a modular environment. This chapter deals with definitions, shows the importance of planning and discusses the efficient development of modular programs. The next chapter deals with the problems of testing with and without a special module tester. The overall aim is not to teach modular programming, which would deserve a book to itself, but to highlight problem areas and to suggest ways in which full use of available aids and facilities may be made. Concepts discussed elsewhere (e.g. use of debugging aids) generally apply in a modular situation also, but within modular programming we need to say a good deal more.

12.1 The reasons for modular programming

To ensure that we are all thinking along the same lines a few basic concepts ought to be defined. To recap, if a program is split into modules, which are written *and tested* quite separately, only being brought together when they have all been tested individually, then that is modular programming. How the program is split into modules is a highly contentious question and many criteria are in vogue: number of decisions, number of statements, core size, and so on. Our definition, for the purpose of this book, is that a module must perform a distinct logical task and be 100% testable.

Why do people use modular techniques? The following quotation states the underlying reasons, at the same time drawing attention to the fact that modular programming brings certain problems with it.

'Modular programming is not a new idea: nor are the problems new which it sets out to solve. Programming for business DP is

113

absurdly difficult and expensive in every way, and the resulting programs are of a dismally low quality. Estimates of project cost and completion date are often little better than guesses; measurement of progress on a single program is almost meaningless; the cost of re-allocating partly completed work is intolerable; *program testing is a casual affair, in which an arbitrary few cases are tried out of the millions of possible cases; production programs continue to display new errors month after month.* [Our italics.] Modular programming is generally supposed to offer a solution to these problems.

'And it can offer a solution, provided that we recognise that it is not in itself the solution; it is simply a fresh problem. A programmer struggling with all the usual difficulties of writing a large non-modular program is not helped by the suggestion that he ought to break it down into a number of modules: that would only introduce new difficulties of designing interfaces, co-ordinating the module design, writing special testing programs, fitting the modules together to make the final product; his present difficulties are pretty bad and there doesn't seem any reason to add to them. So why modular programming? Because the problems it poses are technical problems which can be solved at a general level, once and for all; and when we have solved them we can use the resulting techniques and facilities to solve the more primitive difficulties of programming. We need to develop a detailed technology for modular programming, which will allow us to obtain the benefits that modular programming is supposed to give.'*

The technology for modular programming has now been developed, sufficiently if not fully. The question is how to use it effectively.

12.2 Modular planning

12.2.1 The programming section

The possible effects of modular programming on a programming section were touched upon in Chapter 6 but we would like to discuss them in more detail here. In a fully-modular installation there are differences in responsibilities as compared with a conventional

*From an article in *Computers & Automation*, February 1969, by the Hoskyns Group; quoted with their kind permission.

section because there is far greater polarisation between the senior programmer and the rest of the staff. The senior programmer is a focal point: splitting programs into modules; assigning them to his staff; monitoring their progress; putting together the finished modules; and testing the complete program. He has a varied and interesting job while the junior programmer can easily become a mere coder, with consequent loss of job satisfaction.

2.2.2 Suite planning

Modular programming has no direct impact on the systems analyst. The usual considerations dictate the splitting of a system into programs: program size limitations, use of peripherals, operating considerations, and so on.

2.2.3 Program design

This consists mainly of splitting each program into inter-connecting modules and specifying them: it is the job of the senior programmer. It is important that whatever module definition has been adopted, it must be used consistently. The whole point of modular programming is lost if there are non-standard modules in the system. It would be inappropriate to discuss program-splitting techniques here.

2.2.4 Program documentation

A modular program is rather like a jig-saw puzzle: remove one piece—a module—and only a piece of the same shape can replace it. Modular programming must be well documented if it is to succeed. A precise description of each piece of the jig-saw and its relationships with other pieces is required. There are three principal documentation requirements.

Firstly a clear representation of module inter-relationships is needed such as the diagram given as Figure 12.1. We can see from this which other modules are affected by adding or removing any particular module. For example, if we wanted to include module C in another program we would need to take modules F and G with it.

Then we need to record the internal storage used by the module (i.e. data fields used only within the module) and also the external

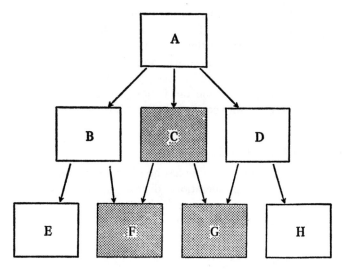

Fig. 12.1 Example module relationship chart

storage requirements (i.e. common to all modules). External storage references are obviously essential to understand fully the relationship between modules. Each item of external data can be used in one of three ways by the module: for modification, for reference or for both. A table such as Figure 12.2 supplements the module relationship chart.

Finally we need a description of what the module is to do, what parameters it will accept, what results it will produce and what subsidiary modules it may call. This document would be the specification for the programmer, as well as an essential piece of long-term documentation.

12.2.5 Programming standards

This subject has been covered at length earlier, but it is worth observing that modular programming lends itself to tight disciplines e.g. standardised data names and procedure labels.

The allocation of modules to programmers is a subject of frequent debate. It may be that the safest rule is never to give any programmer more than one module from the same program, to preclude short

SYSTEM: Part Costing

PROGRAM: PC 019

Variable	A	B	C	D	E			
PAR – 1	M		R		R			
PAR – 2		B	R					
PAR – 3		M	R					
T-DATE				B	R			
T-RTYPE		R	R	B	R			
T-PNO				B				
T-NAME	R			B	R			
T-CUM	R			B	R			
MASTER	R	M	R	R	R			

M = Modified; R = Referenced; B = Both

Fig. 12.2 Example common variable usage

cutting. This would make full and up-to-date documentation essential
and no assumptions could be made. This division is not always
practical and a reasonable compromise is to allocate unrelated
modules to a programmer to minimise interface familiarity.

The programmer should design his own test data for a module, and
this data must test each path. A detailed flowchart showing each
decision-point is useful for plotting the paths to be tested; the

117

number of paths equals the number of items of data necessary to test the module fully. This exhaustiveness is not practical in a monolithic environment but highly practical in a modular one. In fact, it is one of the major virtues of modularity.

12.3 Conclusions

Modular programming was invented to combat the inefficiencies of program development but in the process it introduces a few problems of its own, which we have illustrated. An important problem is how to test modules independently. There are two approaches: to use one of the proprietary module-testing packages or to do without. These two situations will be discussed in the next chapter.

13 Module testing

Where full modular programming is employed, i.e. where modules are tested independently, it is usually the case that a module testing package is used, and this, as we shall see, makes module testing very easy. But we will look first at the testing of a module without using a package because it allows us to lay down a few general principles, and also because it may help those who have to do it, of course. We will then look at the testing of a module using a package and at the extra bonuses that use of a package can give.

13.1 Basic concepts of independent module testing

Whether or not a testing package is used, there are certain principles involved in testing a module independently. Without using a package, following these principles can be arduous and the packages were invented to relieve this effort.

3.1.1 Minimum alterations

The module under test should not be altered (to make it testable) any more than is absolutely necessary, for fairly obvious reasons. Any modification made will have to be un-made at a later stage of development and that process is itself error-prone, and should be avoided as much as possible.

3.1.2 Calling routine

Most modules are called from another module, and it is therefore more natural to test them as called modules, rather than making them free-standing programs. Thus the calling routine will provide the module with its input, and will handle any output produced by it.

This calling module will usually need to be a special one, provided either by the package or by the programmer.

If the programmer provides the calling routine he has a choice between two possibilities:

(a) to take the existing control module of the program and modify it to test only the module required, and possibly to handle program input/output in a different way, as we shall see later;

(b) to write a new calling module that can *only* test the module concerned.

The alternative to provision of a special calling module is to alter the module under test to make it a free-standing program. This would involve inserting coding to handle input/output which would usually be fairly substantial and conflict with the first principle.

13.1.3 Use of debugging aids

Debugging aids may need to be used to monitor the progress of the module, so as to check that intermediate calculations are correct or to trace the path of logically complex routines.

13.1.4 'Bottom-up' approach

The modules should be developed, as far as is practicable, starting at the lowest level and working upwards, except where the testing of a particular module is not dependent upon the functioning of lower modules called by it. One of the major problems of testing modules which call others is that, unless they have been developed already, their processing will have to be simulated in some way to make the test of the higher level module possible. We shall return to this problem shortly.

13.2 Module complexity and testing implications

In Chapter 6 we showed how the monolithic programmer could analyse his program for complexities and so decide upon his testing approach. Similarly, the modular programmer can examine each module to define its testing problems. A module can have the same complexities as a program but may also have a few problems of its own. In any one module the problems are usually few in number simply because all a program's problems are shared between its component modules. Testing problems we distinguish are:

(a) input;
(b) output;
(c) complexities, further subdivided into:
    (i)   file
    (ii) logic
    (iii) arithmetic;
(d) lower-level modules.

Exactly what we mean by these and how we suggest they can be tackled in a module is discussed in the following sections. Figure 13.1 shows where the classes of problems are usually encountered.

An *independent* (or *control*) module is one which is not itself called by any other module but which controls the program by calling the modules at the next lower level. All the other modules of a program are *dependent*, i.e. they depend upon being called by some other module.

Type of Problem	Type of Module	
	Independent (*Control*)	Dependent (*Normal*)
Input	Yes	No
Output	Yes	No
Complexity:		
File	Yes	No
Logical	Perhaps	Yes
Arithmetic	No	Yes
Lower Level Modules	Yes	No

Fig. 13.1 Relationships between type of module and testing problems

121

13.3 Testing without a module testing package

13.3.1 Testing a dependent module

Input problems

It is unusual for a dependent module to have a large volume of input since input/output is usually taken care of by the control module. Any records required by the dependent module are passed to it in the form of parameters and so, for testing, the files in use clearly do not need to be on their actual input medium. This is often a useful point, as records being read in by the dummy control module may be read from cards instead of from disc. Or the dummy control module could simply have the records stored within itself and so need not read any physical file at all.

Output problems

Output produced by dependent modules is usually passed back to the control module for further processing or to be written to a file. When testing a module by itself the output does not need to be actually written to a magentic file, as we only want to examine it. The usual procedure is for the dummy control module to print the output.

Types of complexity

1. File complexity is really a logical problem but is kept separate for ease of recognition. In modular programming it is only really applicable to the control module and will be discussed later.
2. Logical complexity does sometimes occur in modules and when it does it should be monitored by careful use of debugging aids.
3. Arithmetical complexity also arises from time to time and the same monitoring techniques discussed earlier should be used.

Lower level modules

If the lower level modules have already been developed they can simply be linked into the test along with the module being tested.

If they have not yet been developed we must look at the problem of simulating them. Some lower level modules must be present

122

whereas others can validly be bypassed. To bypass a module we might simply just display whatever parameters would have been passed to it and jump around its call. If the omission of the lower level module would render the test useless, then the best solution would be to shelve the test until that module has been developed.

Example

Our example module is arithmetically complex, reads no input files, but receives four input parameters from the control module. The results are stored in two output fields. It also uses a lower level module which would normally be used to print and report upon one intermediate result; this module is not yet written.

Firstly we require a calling module to control our test module. It must be able to provide the required input and handle the output. The input is very low volume and can be generated by the calling module. We then know exactly what the parameter contents will be on entry and from these we can calculate the results which should be output. Because the calculations are complex some intermediate results should be sampled during the test by snapshot prints at strategic positions. In this way the arithmetic can be closely monitored and the actions of the lower level module have in fact been simulated. This module should now be 'dummied out' by inserting a branch around its call. Notes on this and any other extra coding should be kept so that it can be easily removed at the end of the tests. Finally the output parameters can be displayed by the dummy calling module.

3.3.2 Testing a control module

Input

This problem applies far more often to control modules than to lower level modules. Whereas with a dependent module we could have test files in core, etc., now we must have actual files on their proper physical devices.

Output

This problem also applies usually to control modules rather than to lower level ones. Once again the output should now be written to its actual files, which if it is not a print file will need to be printed with a utility.

Types of complexity

1. File complexity frequently applies to control modules because the control module actually reads and writes all of the files. The problem is a logical one and as such is amenable to being monitored by a trace-type facility.
2. Logical complexity usually applies, in the case of a control module, to the logic that decides which modules to call, when, and what action to take on return from them. The run can be monitored by traces and/or snapshot dumps.
3. Arithmetical complexity should never occur in a control module since one of the objectives of the modular approach is to remove this type of complexity to one of the lower level modules.

Lower-level modules

The need to leave the testing of the control module until last is obvious because of the problems that would otherwise arise.

13.4 Testing with a package

13.4.1 Easing the problems

The use of specially designed software to test modules independently can considerably reduce the time and effort spent on the task:

The necessity to alter a module in order to test it is generally removed by a package: it is the main function.

The testing package *is* a standardised calling routine, so the need to write one each time is removed completely.

The idea remains, but using debugging aids is made easier as most module testers provide some facilities of their own.

The need to wait for lower level modules to be developed first is generally removed as most packages have extensive facilities for simulating the action of as-yet undeveloped modules.

Most packages allow sets of test parameters to be input and these

124

are automatically printed before a call is made to a module and any alteration to the parameters (input or output) are printed immediately after module execution.

Some testing packages have associated utilities with which test files can be set up, for testing input or control modules realistically. Output parameters from the module will be printed after execution. The package will allow output files to be created exactly as normal.

3.4.2 Extra bonuses

Some module testing packages are the best examples of what might be called a 'debugging package' in the fullest sense of the words. Besides the basic module testing function they may provide some combination of the following extra facilities:

1. *Test file creation*
   The facilities the package may provide can vary from simple test data dispersion to complex data generation.

2. *Monitoring facilities*
   Packages usually have in-built trace or snapshot abilities and these can be invoked without modifying the program under test.

3. *Multi-test facility*
   Many packages allow several sets of test data to be used and separate tests to be performed on these sets of data, within one test session.

4. *Error correction*
   Some packages provide facilities to intercept program failures that would usually cause a dump to occur and the test to be thrown off. The package will analyse the exception, print details of it, and then try to remedy it before returning to allow the test to continue. For example, if a data exception occurred the package might replace the faulty value with zero before returning, and the continuation of the test may then provide further useful information, thus possibly saving further tests.

5. *File printing*
   Often this is an integral feature of the module tester. Some packages have a powerful extra option: if a lower level module

is being included in the test then the expected results to be achieved by it can be given to the package before execution. These will then be compared with the actual results and any differences will be printed.

13.5 Conclusions

If an installation is quite convinced that it wants to 'go modular' then it clearly should look hard at the advantages—mainly time-saving—that testing packages bring. What we hope we have shown is that it is *not* essential to have one first.

Part V

14 Software errors

The lateness of this discussion does not indicate that we regard the subject as unimportant, but is dictated by the need to maintain a logical order of presentation. Everyone who has been concerned with a DP installation knows that software errors are far from unimportant and can create havoc—they can lose files, waste hours of machine time and weeks of programmers' time.

The basic problem is that one has to assume initially that the software is correct. Because it is a 'black box' it is only usually suspected as a last resort. Almost by definition software bugs are difficult to pinpoint and sometimes even more difficult to get removed. All these factors lead to software errors being dreaded by every installation.

14.1 Definition

We will use a fairly broad definition of software to mean any program not actually written by an installation's own programmers. This definition was deliberately chosen so that, for instance, programs written by a software house would be included; although these are not software in the normal sense, similar problems can be created if they contain errors.

14.2 Origins of software

We will be talking about software provided by both machine manufacturers *and* software houses. It is relevant to deal with both as more and more non-manufacturer software is becoming available due to 'unbundling' by IBM and others.

This 'unbundling' trend—selling hardware and software separately, instead of providing the latter 'free' with the former—affects the user in many ways, one of which is the basic correctness of manufacturer software. In a situation where software is provided as a free service by the manufacturer, there is a strong tendency for him to be cynical about its production. He is essentially in business to make and sell electronic equipment and he must provide software in order to sell his goods. But it is a costly nuisance to him. This can be reflected in his treatment of users, an extreme example being one of the British manufacturers some years ago (now merged), who used not to bother to test revisions to software before issuing them to clients. He let his users find the bugs for him, a clearly intolerable situation for the installations.

In an 'unbundled' situation, the manufacturer is in direct software competition and so cannot afford to antagonise clients. One does sometimes wonder if this is the true, long-term aim of 'unbundling': to enable the manufacturer to drop all software production except the most basic.

14.3 Implications of software errors

14.3.1 Types of software

In this section we discuss the implications of software errors, which vary widely with types of software. The broad types we distinguish are:

1. Compilers.
2. Operating systems, monitors, supervisors, etc.
3. Utility and application packages.
4. Installation subroutines, macros, etc.
5. Programs written by an outside agency.

14.3.2 Compilers

The user is usually completely unaware of what actual machine-code instructions are generated by a compiler. But it is at some point in this object program that a run will fail and the programmer has, initially, to assume that it is his own fault. He has a real problem if, in fact, the compiler he used has generated invalid object code from

128

his valid source program: he is one stage removed from the object program.

There are very few non-manufacturer compilers on the market yet (although one looks forward to them), so most of these comments are aimed at the manufacturer. After operating systems, compilers are probably the second most-used software in an installation, so most manufacturers take a good deal of care to issue them as error-free as possible. But compilers are vast and complex programs and 100% correctness is wishful thinking; we must accept that there will always be compiler bugs.

Errors take two principal forms:

(a) errors that stop the compiler itself during the compilation—at least we know about those immediately; and
(b) code-generation errors, which do not show up until the object program is run.

There is not a great deal that can be done about either type except to summon assistance from whoever wrote the compiler. A useful ploy whilst waiting is to try removing anything 'exceptional' in the source code (e.g. vast data areas, very long datanames, heavy use of a facility usually moderately used, etc.), to see if the compiler is being 'stretched' in some way. This is the most common cause of failure. All compilers have restrictions necessarily built in at both design and programming stages and some of them are never notified in the manual. If checking these possibilities for a particular bug is feasible, it should be tried so as to sidestep the bug.

4.3.3 Operating systems, etc.

The purpose of these programs is to control the flow of work through the machine and generally to run it efficiently. Operating systems, like compilers, are immensely powerful and complex, so the chances of them being bug-free are minimal. We will always have problems with operating systems and the more complex and all-embracing they become, the more complex will be the problems. These problems are almost always time-wasting because they are so difficult to prove. The types of error that we distinguish are:

(a) those purely operational in effect—the operator usually notices

129

them fairly quickly;

(b) only affecting one program; program error is suspected first of all and the programmer has to have a strong case before it is regarded as an operating system bug;

(c) supra-program: these are perhaps the most pernicious of software bugs, because they affect more than one program at once and usually only arise under particular combinations of programs, peripherals, etc., in a multi-programming environment. It is the worst kind of error because it is often so difficult to begin suspecting the operating system, let alone to notice a pattern and then to reproduce that pattern to confirm the suspicion.

Operating systems are the most-used pieces of software, so producers take considerable care to check them out, but bugs (in great quantities) are still certain. At one stage, for instance, IBM was prepared to admit openly that there were about 1000 errors per release in OS/360.*

14.3.4 Utilities and application packages

It is convenient to group this wide range of items—everything from a simple tape copy utility to a gigantic inventory control package— simply because it is difficult to generalise about them. There is the same basic problem as always in that the user has to assume correctness initially. Simple, much-used utilities soon become bug-free but others may be little-used *and* have some complex optional facilities, so that bugs can be latent for a very long time.

14.3.5 Internal subroutines, etc.

Most installations have a collection of internal routines, macros, library procedures, and so on, and their use is to be highly recommended. Luckily, most examples are fairly simple and are frequently used, so the errors will be found quickly. Great care should still be taken before releasing them for general use within the installation.

14.3.6 Programs produced by a software house

Strictly speaking, programs written by a software house for an

*M. E. Hopkins, quoted in *Report of a NATO Software Engineering Conference*, ed. Buxton & Randell, NATO, April 1970.

130

installation (to its own specifications) should not be 'black boxes' to the installation's maintenance programmers. Despite documentation standards supposedly agreed as adequate, they often are.

All software houses worthy of the name should accept a post-completion maintenance clause in their contracts, and DP installations should insist on this and not be afraid to exercise their rights under it.

14.4 When to suspect software

14.4.1 By elimination

Let us look again at the types of error and their approximate proportions:

Operator error	5%
Program(mer) error	90%
Hardware error	1%
Systems error	2%
Software error	2%

This sequence is usually the order of investigation: first of all the circumstances of the run are checked to ensure that correct files have been used, correct procedures followed, etc; most errors are program bugs and most time is spent looking for this type of error; only after a great deal of effort is hardware or software suspected. The reason that software errors are so costly is their time-wasting propensity: when *all else* fails, suspect software.

14.4.2 Through inconsistent results

If the same data is passed through exactly the same program and different results are produced, the cause is almost certainly software.

14.4.3 After new releases

From time to time all manufacturers bring out new releases or versions of their software. The revised software can for a short time be suspected more readily, as it is quite common for programs that were previously working to fail after the new release is introduced.

If a release of a compiler contains a new error it can cause programmers developing new programs to chase errors that are not theirs but the compiler's.

The most serious consequence of new errors in software is the possible delayed-action effect. A new error may be in a low-usage item of software and it may be long after the new release before it appears.

14.5 How to prove it

The only way to prove a software error is to reproduce it, and this may involve a lot of effort and machine time. To do this, it is necessary to recreate the circumstances under which the error occurs, which is a pretty thankless task and which frequently sours the relations between software supplier and user. The user always tends to ask, 'Is it really my responsibility to go to all the trouble of proving this error?' And the supplier—like all programmers— is loathe to accept that his programs can still have bugs in them.

14.6 Interaction of manufacturer and user

This is clearly an important area: you cannot just use software and forget who produced it. It will need maintenance from time to time.

A two-way flow of information is necessary and inefficiencies in the communication between the parties are very common. Problems are rarely clear-cut, and rarely all one side's fault. The user is often in too much of a hurry to blame the manufacturer and the manufacturer is often reluctant to listen to grouses, because he has wasted much time in the past investigating spurious 'software errors'. Neither side is as willing to deal with the other as he should be.

14.6.1 Error reporting—user to manufacturer

There is a wide variation between manufacturers in how they handle reported software errors and in the immediacy and extent of follow-up. Most procedures are characterised by the disincentives that are offered to the user rash enough to report a bug: we seem to be back to the problem of the manufacturer not being very interested in software, and even less interested in errors in it. Or perhaps a deliberate wall is erected to act as a filter to keep out all but the *real* software errors.

The environment of error reporting is always one of emergency. Something has gone wrong and, if it is a production run, there may be all sorts of external pressures to get it corrected as quickly as possible, which is why software is often blamed too early, without going through correct procedures to eliminate other possibilities. But once software is suspected, legitimately or otherwise, what the user wants is immediacy of response. There are three levels of communication between user and manufacturer, of varying degrees of immediacy:

(a) on-site manufacturer personnel;
(b) formal bug-reporting procedures;
(c) user group meetings.

There may be a member of the manufacturer's staff on site when the error occurs. There is no general rule concerning his usefulness in these circumstances and an installation can usually judge pretty quickly for itself. At his best, such a person may well be able to advise specifically on the error or its avoidance or may know the right person to approach (through the 'back-door') in the software team.

Most software errors pass through the formal bug-reporting procedures laid down. All manufacturers aim to provide some sort of telephone service for urgent problems although use of it is commonly discouraged and the user is usually pushed into a formalised (often very complicated) postal service.

An important point to bear in mind in an 'unbundled' situation is that a user may be incurring expense by reporting an error. It would be as well to check first.

Finally we have the user-group meeting that most manufacturers organise (or partake in) rather infrequently. They are an opportunity for users to air grouses of general interest, and manufacturers claim to take notice. Obviously only software capability problems can be raised and they are not of use for specific bugs.

14.6.2 Error reporting–manufacturer to user

All manufacturers have some medium for notifying users of *serious* known software problems and the suggested avoidance procedures. Not all problems are reported, merely those bugs that the manufacturer considers to be serious. Most of the 'circular' documents sent out are reasonably efficient in communicating, but distribution is a problem. It is usually impossible to send an installation only those notices concerning software that it uses, so there is blanket distribution and all installations get all software error notices. This creates a problem for the user, as only a few are directly relevant and someone has to sift out the important ones—we will mention this later.

Generally the service provided is adequate.

14.7 Interaction between software house and user

If a user buys a package from a software house he is in a somewhat stronger position than if he obtains it (free or otherwise) from his manufacturer. The manufacturer is selling at least two types of product but the software house only one. The software industry is highly competitive and every software house is jealous of its reputation. So in general software houses will be more willing to investigate alleged errors in their work than will manufacturers.

If there is a decision to be made between a free manufacturer's package and one bought from a software house, the kind of service one gets from both should be investigated.

14.8 Pre-release testing of software

The user is obviously very interested in how correct his software is to begin with. It is extremely difficult for the producer to 'systems test' software in the same way as other suites of programs. It is usually too complex to test all possible combinations of circumstances.

We are glad to be able to report that the manufacturer who did not test his software revisions at all—but let his users find the errors—is no longer with us, although most DPMs feel from time to time that his ideas linger on!

In addition to fairly thorough internal testing most manufacturers attempt to field-test software in a few 'guinea-pig' installations before issuing it for general use. The same basic procedure is followed by software houses, possibly slightly more vigorously for the reasons discussed earlier.

There are no special techniques used to test software: it is an interesting observation that the logical complexity of our software has increased dramatically over the last ten years but the testing methods remain more or less the same.

14.9 Installation standards

The worst crime an installation can commit in this area is to ignore the notifications of errors flowing from the manufacturer. The flow is heavy and unless the installation appoints someone to be directly responsible for sifting the notices, they quickly end up as a large pile in the Chief Programmer's office.

Obviously it is vital that programmers in the installation should be told about known errors or they may waste a lot of time rediscovering them. Just circulating copies of the manufacturer's notice is generally insufficient by itself: we suggest that, in addition, newly reported errors should be discussed at regular meetings, either as a separate exercise or as part of regular progress meetings. There also needs to be an effective procedure for notifying software bugs or in-efficiencies discovered internally.

If the installation is big enough to support a separate software team, they should be responsible for organising bug notification, the alternative being to appoint someone *who has the time* to perform these important communication duties.

14.10 Summary

It is naive to think that any software will be perfect—errors are inevitable. In fact, they will increase in number as software becomes

F

more complex and all-embracing, especially as the producer's testing techniques are not changing. The use of highly modular techniques might improve the situation but they are not generally in use at present because of the run-time and core-space implications, which are unacceptable in software.

Software producers need to improve and constantly monitor:

> the initial correctness of their products;
> their investigation and correction procedures;
> their information services.

An 'unbundled' manufacturer needs to be competitive and a 'bundled' one cannot avoid responsibility of his software.

On the other hand, users need to be on their toes to spot errors. They must maintain good internal information systems and must feed into them all errors reported, both internal and external.

15 Summary

As we explained in the Preface, this book has grown out of a debugging course. The most pleasing feature of these courses was the amount of common ground that we found with the delegates, most of whom were Chief Programmers. In general they were looking for, and thinking about, practical ways in which to improve the effectiveness of their programmers, and the agreement that we found has reassured them that they were thinking along the right lines. And, of course, it has convinced us that we have achieved our aim: the construction of a highly practical methodology that will improve any programmer's method of working to such an extent that he will produce well-designed, fully debugged, and properly documented programs faster than he does at present.

The word 'practical' occurred twice in the above paragraph, and it was not an accident that it did so, because we have consciously included in this book only those methods that we feel the ordinary programmer—working under the usual pressures in a relatively unsophisticated programming environment—could use with advantage. This has led, perhaps, to a certain lack of novelty, the only completely new idea being the use of 'The Method', and in fact this only formalises the processes that one goes through subconsciously, anyway; so perhaps even The Method is only a new face on an old idea.

We do not apologise for this lack of novelty, because we do not feel that present tools and methods of work are necessarily lacking in any way, but that what is lacking is proper use of the tools and proper application of the methods. Thus we have gone right through the programming task and examined each stage critically to see how it should be done, and what tools are available to help. At all stages we have included detailed descriptions of how to carry out the task under examination, be it the use of debugging aids, coding, testing, or whatever, culminating of course in the case study, which is described

137

precisely as it happened. Another important word has appeared here—*how*: we have described not just *what* to do, but *how* to do it.

In doing this, we surprised ourselves by how much it was possible to improve upon the usual way in which particular tasks are carried out, and we hope that you have been surprised too, because these improved methods are the very heart of the book, and anyone who discards them will get little out of what we have said.

The other important feature of this book is the presentation of the whole of the programming task 'in the round' as it were, and this differs from most books on programming, which generally concentrate on only one or two aspects. By this complete presentation one can see that great advantages are to be gained by smallish improvements on all fronts, as well as by a concentrated assault upon a particular aspect. We therefore regard the methods we describe as a debugging package in the fullest sense of the words, covering as they do the points on bug avoidance as well as those on bug elimination.

So there you have it: a practical, down-to-earth manual of programming. Production of this material has certainly helped us to improve our methods, and we feel certain there is something here to help everybody, be it the individual programmer bent on improvement, or the Chief Programmer striving to get more out of his staff. So give the methods a try, and do let us know how you get on (through the publishers).

1 Appendix
Program specification

1. **Program Function**

    The Input Edit validates the various kinds of card transactions
    entering the system and rejects those which contain errors.
    Invalid transactions are suitably edited and printed.   Other
    valid data is written to a separate tape file.

2. **System Flowchart**

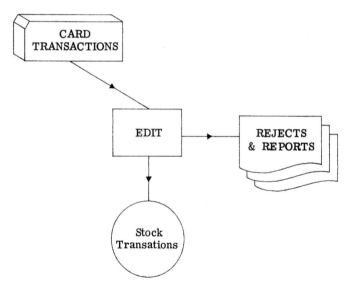

3.   <u>File Contents</u>

3.1   <u>Card Transaction File - Input</u>

    Device :   Card Reader

    Contents : a) Stock Receipts

              b) Stock Returns

              c) Stock Orders (Computer System)

              d) Stock Orders (Manual)

              e) Stock Adjustment (+)

              f) Stock Adjustment (-)

3.2   <u>Stock Transactions File - Output</u>

    Device :   Tape Unit

    Contents : a) Stock Receipts

              b) Stock Returns

              c) Stock Orders (Computer System)

              d) Stock Orders (Manual)

              e) Stock Adjustments

3.3.   <u>Rejects and Reports File</u>

    Device :   Printer

    Contents : a) Rejected Transactions

              b) Transaction Controls

4. Record Formats

4.1 Card File Layouts

Stock Adjustment (+) (e)		15	STOCK NO.	QUANTITY			
Receipt (a)		20	"	"	SUPPLIER NO.		
Return (b)		25	"	"	CUSTOMER NO.	CREDIT NOTE NO.	DATE
Stock Adjustment (-) (f)		30	"	"			
Manual Order (d)		35	"	"	CUSTOMER NO.	DESPATCH NOTE NO.	DATE
Computer Order (c)		45	"	"	"		

4.2 Stock Transaction Layout

Variable length records written in 1500 character blocks
Records layouts are identical to the card formats except
that blank card columns are truncated.

4.3 Rejects and Reports File Layout

As on attached print layout form. Each rejected transaction
produces three lines of print - headings, input data, and
an error line that underscores invalid fields.

142

5.   File Controls

5. 1   Card File

Accumulate counts of:-

a)   transactions input by transaction code.

b)   transactions rejected by transaction code.

c)   One count of invalid transaction codes.

Report counts at end of job.

5. 2   Stock Transactions File

Count the output records by record type (transaction code).
Report the counts at end of job.

6.   Validation

In the specifications the following conventions apply:-

a)   N represents a numeric character

b)   A represents an alphabetic character

c)   C represents a numeric check digit

d)   Seven digit numbers containing check digits in the low
order position use weightings of 7 - 6 - 5 - 4 - 3 - 2,
and a modulus of 11.   Remainder 10 is considered to
be zero.

6. 1   Stock Number

Format   NNNNNNC
Leading spaces not allowed
Must be greater than zero

6. 2   Customer Number and Supplier Number

Format   NNNNNNC
Leading spaces not allowed
Must be greater than zero

6. 3   Quantity

Format   NNNNNN
Leading spaces allowed
Must be greater than zero

6. 4   Credit Note/Despatch Note Number

These reference numbers, raised by the manual system, are required for computer invoicing procedures.

Format   ANNNNNN
No spaces allowed

6. 5   Date

Format   DDMMYY
$00 < MM < 13$
$69 < YY < 90$
$00 < DD < 32$ if MM = 01, 03, 05, 07, 08, 10, 12
$00 < DD < 31$ if MM = 04, 06, 09, 11
$00 < DD < 30$ if MM = 02 and YY divisible by 4
$00 < DD < 29$ if MM = 02 and YY not divisible by 4
First position of day and month allowed to be a space

6. 6   Unused columns

These must all be blanks

2 Appendix
Sample of program listing

```
101      320040        88   STOCK-RECEIPT                          VALUE '20'.
102      320050        88   STOCK-RETURN                           VALUE '25'.
103      320060        88   NEG-ADJUST                             VALUE '30'.
104      320070        88   MAN-ORDER                              VALUE '35'.
105      320080        88   COM-ORDER                              VALUE '45'.
106      320090     03  STOCK-NO                     PICTURE X(7).
107      320100     03  QUANTITY                     PICTURE X(6).
108      320110     03  UNUSED-65-COLS               PICTURE X(65).
109      320120     03  FILLER  REDEFINES UNUSED-65-COLS.
110      320130        05   SUPP-OR-CUST-NO          PICTURE X(7).
111      320140        05   UNUSED-58-COLS           PICTURE X(58).
112      320150        05   FILLER  REDEFINES UNUSED-58-COLS.
113      320160           07   CREDIT-OR-DESP-NO.
114      320170              09   FIRST-CHAR         PICTURE X.
115      320180              09   NUM-PART           PICTURE X(6).
116      320190           07   DATE.
117      320200              09   DAY                PICTURE XX.
118      320210              09   MONTH              PICTURE XX.
119      320211                 88   FEBRUARY                      VALUE '02'.
120      320215              09   NUM-MONTH REDEFINES MONTH PICTURE 99.
121      320220              09   YEAR               PICTURE XX.
122      320225              09   NUM-YEAR  REDEFINES YEAR  PICTURE 99.
123      320230           07   UNUSED-45-COLS        PICTURE X(45).
124      320240
125      330010  01  CHECK-TOTALS      COMPUTATIONAL-3.
126      330020     03  TOTALS-STORE.
127      330030        05   FILLER  OCCURS 3.
128      330040           07   TOTAL-15             PICTURE S9(5).
129      330050           07   TOTAL-20             PICTURE S9(5).
130      330060           07   TOTAL-25             PICTURE S9(5).
131      330070           07   TOTAL-30             PICTURE S9(5).
132      330080           07   TOTAL-35             PICTURE S9(5).
133      330090           07   TOTAL-45             PICTURE S9(5).
134      330100           07   TOTAL-OTHER          PICTURE S9(5).
135      330110           07   TOTAL-OVERALL        PICTURE S9(5).
136      330120     03  TOTALS-ARRAY REDEFINES TOTALS-STORE.
137      330130        05   TOTALS-PART OCCURS 3.
138      330140           07   INDIVIDUAL-TOTAL   OCCURS 7  PICTURE S9(5).
139      330150           07   GRAND-TOTAL                   PICTURE S9(5).
140      330160
141      340010  01  VALIDATION-FLAGS.
142      340020     03 * MAIN-FLAG                   PICTURE   X.
143      340030        88   TRANSACTION-IS-VALID                   VALUE '0'.
144      340040     03  BLANK-FLAG                   PICTURE   X.
145      340050        88   UNUSED-COLS-BLANK                      VALUE '0'.
146      340060     03  TRANS-FLAG                   PICTURE   X.
147      340070        88   INVALID-TRANS-CODE                     VALUE '1'.
148      340080     03  STOCK-NO-FLAG                PICTURE   X.
149      340090        88   INVALID-STOCK-NO                       VALUE '1'.
150      340100     03  QUANT-FLAG                   PICTURE   X.
151      340110        88   INVALID-QUANTITY                       VALUE '1'.
152      340120     03  SUPP-CUST-NO-FLAG            PICTURE   X.
153      340130        88   INVALID-SUPP-CUST-NO                   VALUE '1'.
154      340140     03  CRED-DESP-NO-FLAG            PICTURE   X.
155      340150        88   INVALID-CRED-DESP-NO                   VALUE '1'.
156      340160     03  DATE-FLAG                    PICTURE   X.
```

145

```
157         340170          88  INVALID-DATE                        VALUE '1'.
158         340180      03  NUM-AND-CHECK-FLAG          PICTURE   X.
159         340190      03  NUMERIC-FLAG               PICTURE   X.
160         340200      03  CHECK-DIGIT-FLAG           PICTURE   X.
161         340210
162         341010 01  NUM-TEST-FIELDS.
163         341020      03  SIX-DIGIT.
164         341030          05  FILLER                 PICTURE X     VALUE '0'.
165         341040          05  FIELD-6                PICTURE X(6).
166         341070      03  SEVEN-DIGIT.
167         341080          05  FILLER                 PICTURE X     VALUE '0'.
168         341090          05  FIELD-7.
169         341100              07  DIGIT    OCCURS 6   PICTURE 9.
170         341110              07  CHECK-DIGIT     PICTURE 9.
171         341120          05  FILLER                 PICTURE X     VALUE '0'.
172         341130      03  TEST-FIELD-7    REDEFINES SEVEN-DIGIT   PICTURE X(9).
173         341140
174         341150 01  DAYS-IN-MONTH.
175         341160      03  LAST-DAY.
176         341170          05  FILLER                 PICTURE XX    VALUE '31'.
177         341180          05  FILLER                 PICTURE XX    VALUE '28'.
178         341190          05  FILLER                 PICTURE XX    VALUE '31'.
179         341200          05  FILLER                 PICTURE XX    VALUE '30'.
180         341210          05  FILLER                 PICTURE XX    VALUE '31'.
181         341220          05  FILLER                 PICTURE XX    VALUE '30'.
182         341230          05  FILLER                 PICTURE XX    VALUE '31'.
183         341240          05  FILLER                 PICTURE XX    VALUE '31'.
184         341250          05  FILLER                 PICTURE XX   VALUE '30'.
185         341260          05  FILLER                 PICTURE XX    VALUE '31'.
186         341270          05  FILLER                 PICTURE XX    VALUE '30'.
187         341280          05  FILLER                 PICTURE XX   VALUE '31'.
188         341290      03  MONTH-END    REDEFINES LAST-DAY OCCURS 12
189         341300                                     PICTURE XX.
190         350010 01  PAGE-HEADING.
191         350020      03  FILLER PICTURE X(116) VALUE
192         350030              '                                        STOCK TRA
193         350040-                        'SACTIONS VALIDATION PROGRAM.   REJECTS P
194         350050-                        'PORT.                          PAGE '.
195         350060      03  PAGE-NO PICTURE ZZ9.
196         350070
197         350080 01  ERROR-REPORT-LINES.
198         350090      03  ERROR-HEADING.
199         350100          05  FILLER                 PICTURE X(41) VALUE
200         350110              ' TRANSACTION CODE   STOCK NO.   QUANTITY  '.


251         350620      03  CONTROLS-HEADING-1         PICTURE X(59)  VALUE   ' TRANS
252         350630-          'TIONS INPUT, REJECTED AND OUTPUT WERE AS FOLLOWS--'
253         350640      03  CONTROLS-HEADING-2         PICTURE X(55)  VALUE
254         350650          '  CODE      15    20    25    30    35    45 OTHER     TOTAL'.
255         350660      03  CONTROLS-DETAIL-STRUCTURE.
256         350670          05  FILLER                 PICTURE X(55)  VALUE
257         350680          ' INPUT      9999 9999 9999 9999 9999 9999 9999      99999'.
258         350690          05  FILLER                 PICTURE X(55)  VALUE
259         350700          ' OUTPUT     9999 9999 9999 9999 9999 9999 9999      99999'.
260         350710          05  FILLER                 PICTURE X(55)  VALUE
261         350720          ' REJECTED 9999 9999 9999 9999 9999 9999 9999      99999'.
262         350730      03  CONTROLS-DETAIL-LINE REDEFINES CONTROLS-DETAIL-STRUCTURE
263         350740                                     OCCURS 3.
264         350750          05  FILLER                 PICTURE X(10).
265         350760          05  CONTROL-TOTALS OCCURS 7.
266         350770              07  FILLER             PICTURE X.
267         350780              07  CONTROL-TOTAL      PICTURE ZZZ9.
268         350790          05  FILLER                 PICTURE X(5).
269         350800          05  CONTROL-GRAND-TOTAL PICTURE Z(4)9.
270         350810
271         350820 01  DIAGNOSTIC-SWITCHES.
272         350830      03  SWITCH PICTURE X   OCCURS 80.
273         350840
274         350850
275         400010 PROCEDURE DIVISION.
276         400020
277         400030 DUMMY SECTION.
278         400040 DUMMY-PARA.
279         400050      ACCEPT DIAGNOSTIC-SWITCHES.
280         400060      DISPLAY DIAGNOSTIC-SWITCHES.
```

```
281          400070
282          400080 MAIN SECTION.
283          400090 NOTE-M1.          NOTE THAT THIS SECTION OPENS AND CLOSES FILES, IS
284          400100                    RESPONSIBLE FOR ALL INPUT / OUTPUT OPERATIONS AND
285          400110                    CONTROLS THE PROGRAM FLOW. IT CALLS OTHER SECTIONS
286          400120                    FOR HOUSEKEEPING, VALIDATION, TAPE-EDIT, PRINT-EDIT
287          400130                    AND ACCUMULATION OF CONTROL TOTALS.
288          400140
289          400144 HOUSEKEEP.
290          400145      PERFORM HOUSEKEEPING.
291          400150
292          400160 OPEN-FILES.
293          400170      OPEN INPUT  CARD-FILE
294          400180            OUTPUT TAPE-FILE, PRINT-FILE.
295          400190
296          400200 READ-A-CARD.
297          400210      READ CARD-FILE INTO WS-CARD AT END GO TO END-OF-RUN.
298          400220
299          400230      IF SWITCH (1) IS NOT EQUAL TO SPACE
300          400240            DISPLAY '1/400210 INPUT TRANSCODE ', TRANS-CODE.
301          400250
302          400260      MOVE 1 TO CONTROL-TYPE.
303          400270      PERFORM ACCUMULATION.
304          400280      PERFORM VALIDATION.
305          400290
306          400300      IF SWITCH (1) IS NOT EQUAL TO SPACE
307          400310            DISPLAY '1/400280 ERROR FLAGS ', VALIDATION-FLAGS.
308          400320
309          400330      IF TRANSACTION-IS-VALID
310          400340            THEN PERFORM PROCESS-VALID-TRANS      THRU
311          400350                         PROCESS-VALID-TRANS-END
312          400360            ELSE PERFORM PROCESS-INVALID-TRANS    THRU
313          400370                         PROCESS-INVALID-TRANS-END.
314          400380      GO TO READ-A-CARD.
315          400390
316          400400 END-OF-RUN.
317          400410      MOVE MAX-LINES TO LINE-COUNT.
318          400420      PERFORM CONTROLS-EDIT THRU CONTROLS-EDIT-END.
319          400430      PERFORM PAGEING-ROUTINE THRU PAGEING-ROUTINE-END.
320          400440      PERFORM PRINT-CONTROLS THRU PRINT-CONTROLS-END.
321          400450      CLOSE  CARD-FILE, TAPE-FILE, PRINT-FILE.
322          400460      STOP RUN.
323          400470
324          400480
325          400490 NOTE-M2.          NOTE THAT THE FOLLOWING ROUTINE IS PERFORMED IF
326          400500                    THE INPUT TRANSACTION IS JUDGED BY THE VALIDATION
327          400510                    SECTION TO BE VALID. IT PERFORMS THE ACCUMULATION
328          400520                    AND TAPE EDIT SECTIONS AND FINALLY WRITES THE
329          400530                    CORRECT OUTPUT RECORD TO TAPE.
330          400540
331          400550 PROCESS-VALID-TRANS.
332          400560      MOVE 2 TO CONTROL-TYPE.
333          400570      PERFORM ACCUMULATION.
334          400580      PERFORM TAPE-EDIT.
335          400590      IF  TRANS-L15   WRITE TRANSACTION-L15
336          400600                      GO TO PROCESS-VALID-TRANS-END.
337          400610      IF  TRANS-L22   WRITE TRANSACTION-L22
338          400620                      GO TO PROCESS-VALID-TRANS-END.
339          400630      WRITE TRANSACTION-L35.
340          400640 PROCESS-VALID-TRANS-END.
341          400650      EXIT.
342          400660
343          400670
344          400680 NOTE-M3.          NOTE THAT THE FOLLOWING ROUTINE IS PERFORMED IF
345          400690                    THE INPUT TRANSACTION IS JUDGED BY THE VALIDATION
346          400700                    SECTION TO BE INVALID. IT PERFORMS THE ACCUMULATION
347          400710                    AND PRINT EDIT SECTIONS AND FINALLY PRINTS THE
348          400720                    ERROR REPORT FOR THIS TRANSACTION.
349          400730
350          400740 PROCESS-INVALID-TRANS.


501          700040                    IT OPERATES BY PERFORMING EVER-LOWER ROUTINES THAT
502          700050                    VALIDATE INDIVIDUAL RECORD TYPES OR PARTICULAR
503          700060                    FIELDS.
```

147

```
504        700070
505        700080 NOTE-V2.        NOTE THAT THE FOLLOWING ROUTINE CHECKS TRANSAC
506        700090                 CODES AND PERFORMS THE APPROPRIATE VALIDATION
507        700100                 ROUTINE.
508        700110 VALIDATION-CONTROL.
509        700120
510        700130     MOVE        ZEROES TO VALIDATION-FLAGS.
511        700140
512        700150     IF          POS-ADJUST OR NEG-ADJUST
513        700160         THEN PERFORM VALIDATE-ADJUSTS       THRU
514        700170                      VALIDATE-ADJUSTS-END,
515        700180              GO TO    VALIDATION-END,
516        700190         ELSE NEXT SENTENCE.
517        700200
518        700210     IF          STOCK-RECEIPT OR COM-ORDER
519        700220         THEN PERFORM VALIDATE-REC-OR-COM-ORDER     THRU
520        700230                      VALIDATE-REC-OR-COM-ORDER-END,
521        700240              GO TO    VALIDATION-END,
522        700250         ELSE NEXT SENTENCE.
523        700260
524        700270     IF          STOCK-RETURN OR MAN-ORDER
525        700280         THEN PERFORM VALIDATE-RET-OR-MAN-ORDER     THRU
526        700290                      VALIDATE-RET-OR-MAN-ORDER-END,
527        700300              GO TO    VALIDATION-END,
528        700310         ELSE NEXT SENTENCE.
529        700320
530        700330     NOTE;       *** INVALID TRANSACTION CODE ***.
531        700340     MOVE        'I' TO MAIN-FLAG, TRANS-FLAG.
532        700350     PERFORM     VALIDATE-INVALID-TRANS     THRU
533        700360                 VALIDATE-INVALID-TRANS-END.
534        700370     GO TO       VALIDATION-END.
535        700380
536        700390 NOTE-V3.        NOTE THAT THE FOLLOWING ROUTINE VALIDATES STOCK
537        700400                 ADJUSTMENTS.  IT OPERATES BY PERFORMING ROUTINE
538        700410                 THAT VALIDATE PARTICULAR FIELDS.
539        700420 VALIDATE-ADJUSTS.
540        700430
541        700440     PERFORM     VALIDATE-STOCK-NO     THRU
542        700450                 VALIDATE-STOCK-NO-END.
543        700460     PERFORM     VALIDATE-QUANTITY     THRU
544        700470                 VALIDATE-QUANTITY-END.
545        700480     MOVE        UNUSED-65-COLS TO BLANK-TEST-FIELD.
546        700490     PERFORM     VALIDATE-UNUSED-COLS     THRU
547        700500                 VALIDATE-UNUSED-COLS-END.
548        700510
549        700520 VALIDATE-ADJUSTS-END.
550        700530     EXIT.


601        701050     PERFORM     VALIDATE-QUANTITY     THRU
602        701060                 VALIDATE-QUANTITY-END.
603        701070     MOVE        UNUSED-45-COLS TO BLANK-TEST-FIELD.
604        701080     PERFORM     VALIDATE-UNUSED-COLS     THRU
605        701090                 VALIDATE-UNUSED-COLS-END.
606        701100
607        701110 VALIDATE-INVALID-TRANS-END.
608        701120     EXIT.
609        701130
610        701140 NOTE-V7.        NOTE THAT THE FOLLOWING ROUTINE VALIDATES STOCK
611        701150                 NUMBERS.  IT OPERATES BY PERFORMING A ROUTINE T
612        701160                 VALIDATES THE TWO PARTS OF THE NUMBER.
613        701170 VALIDATE-STOCK-NO.
614        701180
615        701190     MOVE        STOCK-NO TO FIELD-7.
616        701200
617        701210         IF   SWITCH (2) NOT EQUAL TO SPACE, DISPLAY '2/701210
618        701220              'S.NO=' STOCK-NO, 'V.F=' FIELD-7,
619        701230              'FLAGS=' VALIDATION-FLAGS.
620        701240
621        701530
622        701250     PERFORM     VALIDATE-NUM-AND-CHECK          THRU
623        701260                 VALIDATE-NUM-AND-CHECK-END.
624        701270     IF          NUM-AND-CHECK-FLAG EQUAL TO ZEROS
625        701280         THEN GO TO VALIDATE-STOCK-NO-END,
626        701290         ELSE NEXT SENTENCE.
```

SEQ ERR (line 622)

148

```
627    701300    NOTE;      *** INVALID FIELD ***.
628    701310    MOVE       '1' TO MAIN-FLAG, STOCK-NO-FLAG.
629    701320
630    701330 VALIDATE-STOCK-NO-END.
631    701340
632    701350         IF  SWITCH (2) NOT EQUAL TO SPACE, DISPLAY '2/701350 ',
633    701360             'S. NO=' STOCK-NO, 'V. F=' FIELD-7,
634    701370             'FLAGS=' VALIDATION-FLAGS.
635    701380
636    701390 NOTE-V8.      NOTE THAT THE FOLLOWING ROUTINE VALIDATES
637    701400               QUANTITIES. IT OPERATES BY FIRST REPLACING LEADING
638    701410               SPACES BY ZEROS AND THEN PERFORMING A NUMERIC
639    701420               VALIDATION.
640    701430 VALIDATE-QUANTITY.
641    701440
642    701450     EXAMINE   QUANTITY,
643    701460         REPLACING LEADING SPACES BY ZEROS.
644    701470     MOVE      QUANTITY TO FIELD-6.
645    701480     MOVE      SIX-DIGIT TO FIELD-7.
646    701490
647    701500         IF  SWITCH (3) NOT EQUAL TO SPACE, DISPLAY '3/701500 ',
648    701510             'QTY=' IC-QUANTITY, 'V. F=' FIELD-7,
649    701520             'FLAGS=' VALIDATION-FLAGS.
650    701540     PERFORM   VALIDATE-NUMERIC       THRU


701    702040               'FLAGS=' VALIDATION-FLAGS.
702    702050
703    702060     IF        FIRST-CHAR EQUAL TO SPACE
704    702070         OR FIRST-CHAR NOT ALPHABETIC,
705    702080         THEN  GO TO SET-CRED-DESP-NO-FLAG,
706    702090         ELSE  NEXT SENTENCE.
707    702100
708    702110     NOTE;     *** VALID FIRST CHARACTER ***.
709    702120     PERFORM   VALIDATE-NUMERIC       THRU
710    702130               VALIDATE-NUMERIC-END.
711    702140     IF        NUMERIC-FLAG EQUAL TO ZEROS,
712    702150         THEN  GO TO VALIDATE-CREDIT-OR-DESP-NO-END,
713    702160         ELSE  NEXT SENTENCE.
714    702170
715    702180     NOTE;     *** INVALID FIELD ***.
716    702190
717    702200 SET-CRED-DESP-NO-FLAG.
718    702210
719    702220     MOVE      '1' TO MAIN-FLAG, CRED-DESP-NO-FLAG.
720    702230
721    702240 VALIDATE-CREDIT-OR-DESP-NO-END.
722    702250
723    702260         IF  SWITCH (5) NOT EQUAL TO SPACE, DISPLAY '5/702260 ',
724    702270             'C/D=' CREDIT-OR-DESP-NO, 'V. F=' FIELD-7,
725    702280             'FLAGS=' VALIDATION-FLAGS.
726    702281
727    702282 NOTE-V11.     NOTE THAT THE FOLLOWING ROUTINE VALIDATES DATES.
728    702283               IT OPERATES BY FIRST REPLACING LEADING SPACES IN
729    702284               DAY AND MONTH, THEN PERFORMING A NUMERIC VALIDATION
730    702285               ON THE WHOLE DATE, AND FINALLY CHECKING THE DATE AS
731    702286               SUCH, USING A TABLE OF DAYS IN THE MONTH THAT HAS
732    702287               28: AS THE LAST DAY OF FEBRUARY.
733    702300 VALIDATE-DATE.
734    702310
735    702320     EXAMINE   DAY,
736    702330         REPLACING LEADING SPACE BY ZERO.
737    702340     EXAMINE   MONTH,
738    702350         REPLACING LEADING SPACE BY ZERO.
739    702360     MOVE      DATE TO FIELD-6.
740    702370     MOVE      SIX-DIGIT TO FIELD-7.
741    702380
742    702390         IF  SWITCH (6) NOT EQUAL TO SPACE, DISPLAY '6/702390 ',
743    702400             'DATE=' DATE, 'V. F=' FIELD-7,
744    702410             'FLAGS=', VALIDATION-FLAGS.
745    702420
746    702430     PERFORM   VALIDATE-NUMERIC       THRU
747    702440               VALIDATE-NUMERIC-END.
748    702450     IF        NUMERIC-FLAG NOT EQUAL TO ZEROS,
749    702460         THEN  GO TO SET-DATE-FLAG,
750    702470         ELSE  NEXT SENTENCE.
```

149

```
751          702480
752          702490     NOTE:      *** VALID NUMERIC ***.
753          702510     IF         YEAR GREATER THAN '89' OR YEAR LESS THAN '70',
754          702520          THEN  GO TO SET-DATE-FLAG,
755          702530          ELSE  NEXT SENTENCE.
756          702540
757          702560     IF         MONTH GREATER THAN '12' OR MONTH LESS THAN '01',
758          702570          THEN  GO TO SET-DATE-FLAG,
759          702580          ELSE  NEXT SENTENCE.
760          702590
761          702610     IF         DAY LESS THAN '01',
762          702620          THEN  GO TO SET-DATE-FLAG,
763          702630          ELSE  NEXT SENTENCE.
764          702640
765          702650     MOVE       MONTH-END (NUM-MONTH) TO MAX-DAYS.
766          702660
767          702670          IF  SWITCH (6) NOT EQUAL TO SPACE, DISPLAY '6/702670 *
768          702680               'DATE=' DATE, 'V.F=' FIELD-7,
769          702690               'MAX-DAYS=' MAX-DAYS.
770          702700
771          702710     IF         DAY NOT GREATER THAN MAX-DAYS,
772          702720          THEN  GO TO VALIDATE-DATE-END,
773          702730          ELSE  NEXT SENTENCE.
774          702740
775          702750     IF         NOT FEBRUARY
776          702760          THEN  GO TO SET-DATE-FLAG,
777          702770          ELSE  NEXT SENTENCE.
778          702780
779          702790     NOTE:      *** THE DATE IS EITHER 29, 30, ETC OF FEBRUARY *
780          702800
781          702810     IF         DAY GREATER THAN '29',
782          702820          THEN  GO TO SET-DATE-FLAG,
783          702830          ELSE  NEXT SENTENCE.
784          702840
785          702850     NOTE:      *** THE DATE IS 29 FEB, BUT IS IT A LEAP YEAR **
786          702860     MOVE       NUM-YEAR TO COMP-YEAR.
787          702865     DIVIDE     4 INTO COMP-YEAR GIVING LY-TEST-FIELD.
788          702866     MULTIPLY   4 BY LY-TEST-FIELD.
789          702867     SUBTRACT   LY-TEST-FIELD FROM COMP-YEAR GIVING LY-TEST-FIEL
790          702870     IF         LEAP-YEAR
791          702880          THEN  GO TO VALIDATE-DATE-END,
792          702890          ELSE  NEXT SENTENCE.
793          702900
794          702910 SET-DATE-FLAG.
795          702920
796          702930     MOVE       '1' TO MAIN-FLAG, DATE-FLAG.
797          702940
798          702950 VALIDATE-DATE-END.
799          702960
800          702970          IF  SWITCH (6) NOT EQUAL TO SPACE, DISPLAY '6/702970 '


851          703470
852          703480          IF  TEST-FIELD-7 IS NOT NUMERIC GO TO SET-NUM-FLAG.
853          703490          IF  FIELD-7 IS GREATER THAN ZEROES GO TO
854          703500                                   VALIDATE-NUMERIC-END.
855          703510 SET-NUM-FLAG.
856          703520     MOVE '1' TO NUMERIC-FLAG.
857          703530 VALIDATE-NUMERIC-END.
858          703550
859          703560          IF SWITCH (8) IS NOT EQUAL TO SPACE
860          703570          DISPLAY '8/703540 FLD7=', FIELD-7, ' FLAGS=',
861          703580                       VALIDATION-FLAGS.
862          703590
863          703600
864          703610 NOTE-V15.    NOTE THAT THE FOLLOWING ROUTINE CALCULATES A
865          703620             CHECK DIGIT FROM THE FIRST SIX DIGITS OF A SEVEN
866          703630             DIGIT NUMBER AND CHECKS THAT THE SEVENTH DIGIT
867          703640             CORRESPONDS.
868          703650
869          703660 VALIDATE-CHECK-DIGIT.
870          703670     MOVE ZERO TO CHECK-DIGIT-FLAG, RESULT.
871          703680     MOVE 1 TO COUNT.
872          703690     MOVE 7    TO MULTIPLIER.
873          703700
```

150

```
874        703710          IF  SWITCH (9) IS NOT EQUAL TO SPACE
875        703720          DISPLAY '9/703690 FLD7=', FIELD-7, ' M=', MULTIPLIER,
876        703730              ' C=', COUNT, ' R=', RESULT, ' FLAGS='
877        703740              VALIDATION-FLAGS.
878        703750
879        703760 CHECK-DIGIT-LOOP.
880        703770     MULTIPLY DIGIT (COUNT) BY MULTIPLIER GIVING INTERMEDIATE.
881        703780     ADD INTERMEDIATE TO RESULT.
882        703790     ADD  1 TO COUNT.
883        703800     IF COUNT IS GREATER THAN 6 GO TO CALC-CHECK-DIGIT.
884        703810     SUBTRACT 1 FROM MULTIPLIER.
885        703820     GO TO CHECK-DIGIT-LOOP.
886        703830 CALC-CHECK-DIGIT.
887        703840
888        703850          IF  SWITCH (9) IS NOT EQUAL TO SPACE
889        703860          DISPLAY '9/703830 FLD7=', FIELD-7, ' M=', MULTIPLIER,
890        703870              ' C=', COUNT, ' R=', RESULT, 'FLAGS=',
891        703880              VALIDATION-FLAGS.
892        703890
893        703900     DIVIDE 11 INTO RESULT GIVING INTERMEDIATE.
894        703910     MULTIPLY 11 BY INTERMEDIATE.
895        703920     SUBTRACT INTERMEDIATE FROM RESULT.
896        703930
897        703940          IF  SWITCH (9) IS NOT EQUAL TO SPACE
898        703950          DISPLAY '9/703920 FLD7=', FIELD-7, ' INTR=',
899        703960              INTERMEDIATE, ' RSLT=', RESULT.
900        703970
901        703980     IF RESULT IS EQUAL TO 10 MOVE ZERO TO RESULT.
902        703990     IF RESULT IS NOT EQUAL TO CHECK-DIGIT MOVE '1' TO
903        704000                                CHECK-DIGIT-FLAG.
904        704010 VALIDATE-CHECK-DIGIT-END.
905        704020
906        704030          IF  SWITCH (9) IS NOT EQUAL TO SPACE
907        704040          DISPLAY '9/704010 FLD7=', FIELD-7, ' RSLT=', RESULT,
908        704050              ' FLAGS=', VALIDATION-FLAGS.
909        704060
910        704080 VALIDATION-END.
911        704100     NOTE;   END OF VALIDATION SECTION.
912        800010
913        800020 TAPE-EDIT SECTION.
914        800030
915        800040 NOTE-T1.        NOTE THAT THIS SECTION DECIDES THE LENGTH OF A
916        800050                 VALID TRANSACTION AND MOVES THE RELEVANT PART OF
917        800060                 THE TRANSACTION CARD TO THE TAPE FILE OUTPUT AREA.
918        800070
919        800080 BEGIN-TAPE-EDIT.
920        800090     IF  POS-ADJUST    OR NEG-ADJUST
921        800100         MOVE WS-CARD TO TRANSACTION-L15
922        800110         MOVE 15     TO TRANS-LENGTH
923        800120         GO TO END-TAPE-EDIT.
924        800130     IF  STOCK-RECEIPT OR COM-ORDER
925        800140         MOVE WS-CARD TO TRANSACTION-L22
926        800150         MOVE 22     TO TRANS-LENGTH
927        800160         GO TO END-TAPE-EDIT.
928        800170     MOVE WS-CARD TO TRANSACTION-L35.
929        800180     MOVE 35     TO TRANS-LENGTH.
930        800190 END-TAPE-EDIT.
931        800200
932        800210 NOTE-T2.       NOTE THAT THIS IS THE END OF THE TAPE EDIT SECTION.
933        800220
934        900010
935        900020 PRINT-EDIT SECTION.
936        900030
937        900040 NOTE-P1.       NOTE THAT THIS SECTION IS CALLED FROM THE MAIN
938        900050               SECTION AND CONSTRUCTS THE REJECT REPORT LINES
939        900060               FOR AN INVALID TRANSACTION. THREE LINES ARE
940        900070               CONSTRUCTED; A HEADING, THE INVALID CARD AND
941        900080               UNDERLINING OF THE INVALID FIELDS.
942        900085               THE HEADING AND INVALID CARD RECORD AREAS ARE SO
943        900087               STRUCTURED THAT SPACE FILLING IS UNNECESSARY.
944        900090                          .
945        900100 BEGIN-PRINT-EDIT.
946        900110     IF  POS-ADJUST    OR NEG-ADJUST
947        900120         PERFORM EDIT-ADJUSTMENT THRU EDIT-ADJUSTMENT-END
948        900130         GO TO END-PRINT-EDIT.
949        900140     IF  STOCK-RECEIPT OR COM-ORDER
950        900150         PERFORM EDIT-RECEIPT-OR-COM-ORDER THRU
```

151

3 Appendix
Macro flowchart

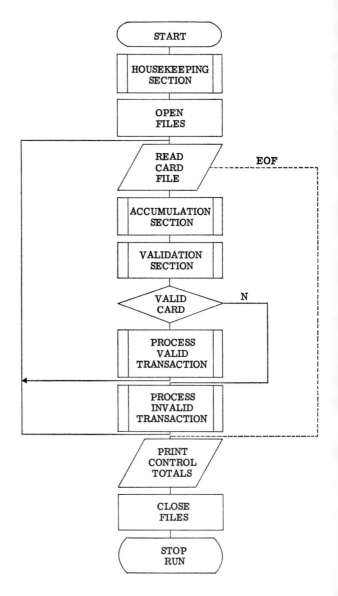

4 Appendix

Sample of automatic flowchart

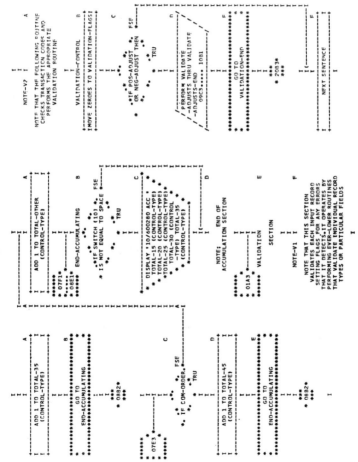

153

SYSTEM OUTPUT EXAMPLES

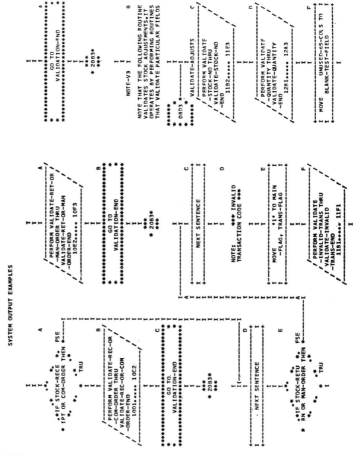

5 Appendix

Cross-reference listing

LABEL CROSS REFERENCE BY ALPHABETIC

LABEL	SEQ #	LOC	REFERENCE BY LOC
ACCUMULATION	600020 S	006E3	001F2,002F2,003E1
BEGIN-ACCUMULATING	600090	007A1	
REGIN-PRINT-EDIT	900100	021A3	
REGIN-TAPE-EDIT	800080	021E3	
CALC-CHECK-DIGIT	703830	020A1	019C3
CHECK-DIGIT-LOOP	703760	019F2	019E3
COMMON-EDIT-TASKS	900880	024E3	022D2,023C1,023C3,024C2
COMMON-EDIT-TASKS-END	900940	025C1	022D2,023C1,023C3,024C2
CONTROL-EDIT-LOOP	400950	003F3	004B1,004C2
CONTROLS-EDIT	400930	003I3	0002L
CONTROLS-EDIT-END	401050	00402	002D1,004A2
DUMMY	400030 S	001A1	
DUMMY-PARA	400040	001B1	
EDIT-ADJUSTMENT	900290	022D2	021B3
EDIT-ADJUSTMENT-END	900350	023A1	021B3
EDIT-INVALID-TRANS-CODE	900720	022C2	022A2
EDIT-INVALID-TRANS-CODE-END	900790	024C3	022A2
EDIT-RECEIPT-OR-COM-ORDER	900410	023C1	021E3
EDIT-RECEIPT-OR-COM-ORDER-END	900490	023A3	021E3
EDIT-RETURN-OR-MAN-ORDER	900550	023C3	022C1
EDIT-RETURN-OR-MAN-ORDER-END	900650	024A2	022C1
END-ACCUMULATING	900780	008B2	007F1,007C2,007A3,007D3,008B1,008E1
END-OF-RUN	400400	002C1	00182
END-PRINT-EDIT	901210	026E2	021C3,022A1,022D1,022B2
END-TAPE-EDIT	800190 S	021C2	021A1,021E1
ERROR-UNDERLINING	901000	025E1	022F3,023F2,024G1,02483
ERROR-UNDERLINING-END	901150	02602	022F3,023F2,024G1,02483,026A1,026D1,026R2
HOUSEKEEP	400144	001F1	
HOUSEKEEPING	500055 S	006F1	001F1
MAIN	400080	00101	
NOTE-A1	600040	006F3	
NOTE-H1	500020	006C1	
NOTE-H2	500180	006D3	
NOTE-M1	400090	001E1	
NOTE-M2	400490	00202	
NOTE-M3	400680	003C1	
NOTE-M4	400890	00303	
NOTE-M5	401090	004E2	
NOTE-M6	401250	005D1	
NOTE-M6A	401424	00503	
NOTE-M7	401440	006A1	
NOTE-P1	900040	021F2	
NOTE-P2	900260	022C2	
NOTE-P3	900380	02381	
NOTE-P4	900520	02383	
NOTE-P5	900680	02482	
NOTE-P6	900820	02403	
NOTE-P7	900970	02501	
NOTE-T1	800040	02003	
NOTE-T2	800210	021D2	
NOTE-V1	700020	008F2	
NOTE-V10	701742	013C2	
NOTE-V12	702832	01742	
NOTE-V13	703000	01783	
NOTE-V14	703120	01802	
NOTE-V15	703380	019E1	
NOTE-V2	700080	008A3	

6 Appendix
Test plan

General Strategy

Testing to be done in stages, aiming to verify most of the program quickly, and hence cut out debug prints early on. More complicated and bulk testing will follow later. Three test packs - simple, complex and utter rubbish (object deck.)

Module Testing Strategy

Program modularized, but modules not tested independently. Can still use modular techniques, like analysis of number of paths in a module and so reduce amount of test data.

Input data

No problem; on cards.

Use of test aids

Modularization will make program much easier to test; fewer logical trickeries. Most of the routines will do one or more of three reasonably simple tasks:

a)   Move data from one field to another.
b)   Call lower level routines.
c)   Make relatively simple tests and act accordingly.

This means that only snapshots will really be required, used to show the input to, and output from a routine. In only two cases will routines need 'tracing' within them, check digit calculation, and date checking.

Expected results schedule

To be provided later.

156

7 Appendix
Expected results schedule

Expected Results schedule - First Test Pack

15 ⎫
20 ⎬ all valid
25 ⎭
30   inv. st. no   inv. blanks
35   in .qty.
40 (inv. trans.)   inv. blanks
45   inv. cust. no   inv. blanks
30 ⎫
35 ⎬ all valid
45 ⎭
25   inv. cr. no.
35   inv des no.   inv. data   inv. blanks
71

Expected Results Schedule - Second Test pack

page 1

TRANSACTION	CODE	STOCK N°	QUANTITY	UNUSED
INVALID	bb	1234560	000001	
INVALID	00	1234560	000001	____ _____
	A9			
Same	4E	Same		
	40			
ADJUST (+)	15	1234561	000001	
		1234560		
Same		b234560	Same	
		1234560		
		XYZA000		
		1235450	000001	

page 2

ADJUST (+)	15	1234560	--------	
--------	Same	--------	-100	
			10E	
			000001	0 ----------
-----------	Same	-----------		AINT BLANK

157

8 Appendix
Program development log

PROGRAM DEVELOPMENT LOG

PROGRAMMER W.A.Sampson / EVENT OR ACTIVITY	PROGRAM NO. Sample / DATE OR DATES	PROGRAM NAME Stock update input edit / ACTION OR RESULTS	SYSTEM Stock Control / NEXT STEP	PAGE 1 of 4 — TIME TAKEN MAN (DAYS)	M/C (MINS)
Received and studied spec.	25.6.71	No queries - spec. approved.	Initial design	¼	
Initial program design.	26.6.71 to 27.6.71	Decided on overall program logic and on the modularization to be adopted.	Test plan	1	
Designing test plan.	28.6.71	Analysis of initial design revealed no great testing problems. Simple input, and only two routines of any complexity	Flowcharting	½	
Flowcharting	28.6.71 to 30.6.71	Completed roughly drawn detailed flowcharts	Use of debugging aids	2	
Use of debugging aids.	30.6.71 to 1.7.71	Simple, modular program design should make testing easy. Analysed each routine and marked on flowchart where and how to use snapshots. No trace required.	Test data and expected results	1	

PROGRAM DEVELOPMENT LOG

PROGRAMMER W.A. Sampson	PROGRAM NO. Sample	PROGRAM NAME Stock update input edit	SYSTEM Stock control	PAGE 2 of 4	
				TIME TAKEN	
EVENT OR ACTIVITY	DATE OR DATES	ACTION OR RESULTS	NEXT STEP	MAN (DAYS)	M/C (MINS)
Test data and expected results	1.7.71 to 2.7.71	Analysed modules and designed a first test pack for an initial, relatively simple, test of most program paths. Should enable verification of most routines. Did rough expected results schedule.	Coding	1	
Coding	2.7.71 to 5.7.71	Coded program	Desk checking	1½	
Desk checking Neal's part of program.	6.7.71	Found several periods omitted, one dataname wrongly spelt, and one paragraph name wrongly spelt twice.	Dry-running	1	
Dry running with first test pack.	7.7.71	7 errors found and corrected. 1. Totals not initialized. 2. INTERMEDIATE too small. 3. Illegal comparison – COMP & X 4. Multiply with X field 5. Examine FIRST not LEADING in date 6. Illegal move X to COMP. 7. Wrong spelling of a dataname.	Efficiency improvement	1	

PROGRAM DEVELOPMENT LOG

PROGRAMMER W.A.Sampson	PROGRAM NO. Sample	PROGRAM NAME Stock update input edit	SYSTEM Stock control	PAGE 3 of 4	
EVENT OR ACTIVITY	DATE OR DATES	ACTION OR RESULTS	NEXT STEP	TIME TAKEN MAN (DAYS)	M/C (MINS)
Improving efficiency	8.7.71	Changed usage of a number of fields from COMP to COMP-3, etc. Improving printing efficiency by using WRITE AFTER dataname option.	Card listing and checking	1	—
Card listing and checking.	9.7.71	Several errors found and duly corrected.	First compn.		2
1st. compilation	9.7.71	A number of C & E errors, so no execution. Errors duly corrected - involved insertion of a housekeeping section to zeroize some totals	Second compn. (& first test?)	1	5
2nd. compilation and 1st. test.	9.7.71	24 warnings, so exec. Got debug prints, but nothing else printed, no records written. Errors written up elsewhere.	Corrected errors		
Error correction	12.7.71	Errors corrected	3rd. compilation and 2nd. test.	½	—

PROGRAM DEVELOPMENT LOG

PROGRAMMER W.A.Sampson	PROGRAM NO. Sample	PROGRAM NAME Stock update input edit	SYSTEM Stock control	PAGE 4 of 4	
EVENT OR ACTIVITY	DATE OR DATES	ACTION OR RESULTS	NEXT STEP	TIME TAKEN MAN (DAYS)	TIME TAKEN M/C (MINS)
3rd. compilation and 2nd. test.	12.7.71	24 warning messages, so exec. went right through first test pack and wrote disc, no errors found.	3rd. test with 2nd. test pack. Main and date switches still on.	1	10
4th. compilation and 3rd. test.	13.7.71	Date error - leap year calculation wrong due to holding decimals in intermediate field. Error written up elsewhere.	Correct error		10
Correct error	13.7.71	Error corrected.	4th. test - all test packs, no switches on.	1	
5th. compilation 4th. test	13.7.71	Correct execution.	Remove debugging aids.		10

9 Appendix
First test

```
// ASSGN    SYS004,X'00C'
// ASSGN    SYS006,X'00E'
// ASSGN    SYS010,X'131'
// DLBL     SYS010,'STOCK TRANSACTIONS FILE',,SD
// EXTENT   SYS010,111111,1,0,200,600
// EXEC

1111111111
1/400210 INPUT TRANSCODE 15
10/600090 ACC   )  )  )  )  )  )  )  )
10/600280 ACC   *  )  )  )  )  )  )  )  *
2/701210 S.NO=1234560V.F=1234560FLAGS=
7/703170 FLD7=1234560 FLAGS=            )
8/703420 FLD7=1234560 FLAGS=           ))
8/703540 FLD7=1234560 FLAGS=           ))
9/703690 FLD7=1234560 M=7 C=1 R=000 FLAGS=        )))
9/703830 FLD7=1234560 M=2 C=7 R=077FLAGS=        .)))
9/703920 FLD7=1234560 INTR=077 RSLT=000
9/704010 FLD7=1234560 RSLT=000 FLAGS=          )))
7/703320 FLD7=1234560 FLAGS=           )))
2/701350 S.NO=1234560V.F=1234560FLAGS=          )))
3/701500 QTY=000001V.F=0000001FLAGS=          )))
8/703420 FLD7=0000001 FLAGS=           )))
8/703540 FLD7=0000001 FLAGS=           )))
3/701650 QTY=000001V.F=0000001FLAGS=          )))
1/400280 ERROR FLAGS              )))
```

162

10 Appendix
Second test

STOCK TRANSACTIONS VALIDATION PROGRAM.   REJECTS REPORT.

```
TRANSACTION CODE    STOCK NO.    QUANTITY                UNUSED PART OF CARD
ADJUST(-)   30       345A314        47
                     -------       -----
                                                         ----------------------

1/400210 INPUT TRANSCODE 35
10/600090 ACC 000010000100001000010000000000000004
10/600280 ACC 000010000100001000010001000000000005
2/701210 S.NO=9876510V.F=9876510FLAGS=00000000000
7/703170 FLD7=9876510 FLAGS=00000000000
8/703420 FLD7=9876510 FLAGS=00000000000
8/703540 FLD7=9876510 FLAGS=00000000000
9/703690 FLD7=9876510 M=7 C=1 R=000 FLAGS=00000000000
9/703830 FLD7=9876510 M=2 C=7 R=187FLAGS=00000000000
9/703920 FLD7=9876510 INTR=187 RSLT=000
9/704010 FLD7=9876510 RSLT=000 FLAGS=00000000000
7/703320 FLD7=9876510 FLAGS=00000000000
2/701350 S.NO=9876510V.F=009 126FLAGS=00000000000
3/701500 QTY= 9 126V.F=009 126FLAGS=00000000000
8/703420 FLD7=009 126 FLAGS=00000000000
8/703540 FLD7=009 126 FLAGS=00000000010
3/701650 QTY= 9 126V.F=009 126FLAGS=10001000010
4/701750 S/C=9876558V.F= 9876558FLAGS=10001000010
7/703170 FLD7=9876558 FLAGS=10001000010
8/703420 FLD7=9876558 FLAGS=10001000000
8/703540 FLD7=9876558 FLAGS=10001000000
9/703690 FLD7=9876558 M=7 C=1 R=000 FLAGS=10001000000
9/703830 FLD7=9876558 M=2 C=7 R=195FLAGS=10001000000
9/703920 FLD7=9876558 INTR=187 RSLT=008
```

163

```
9/704010  FLD7=9876558  RSLT=008  FLAGS=10001000000
7/703320  FLD7=9876558  FLAGS=10001000000
4/701900  S/C=9876558VV  F=9876558FLAGS=10001000000
5/702030  C/D= A302617V.F=0302617FLAGS=10001000000
8/703420  FLD7=0302617  FLAGS=10001000000
8/703540  FLD7=0302617  FLAGS=10001000000
5/702260  C/D=A302617V.F=0302617FLAGS=10001000000
6/702390  DATE=010670V.F=0010670FLAGS=10001000000
8/703420  FLD7=0010670  FLAGS=10001000000
8/703540  FLD7=0010670  FLAGS=10001000000
6/702670  DATE=010670V.F=0010670MAX-DAYS=30
6/702970  DATE=010670VF F= 0010670FLAGS=10001000000
1/400280  ERROR FLAGS 10001000000
10/600090 ACC  000000000000000000010000000000000000000001
10/600280 ACC  000000000000000000010000010000000000000002
```

TRANSACTION CODE	STOCK NO.	QUANTITY	CUSTOMER	DESPCH NO.	DATE
MAN-ORDER 35	9876510	9 126	9876558	A302617	01 670

```
1/400210 INPUT TRANSCODE 40
10/600090 ACC  000010000100001000010000100000000000000005
10/600280 ACC  000010000100001000010000100000000000100006
2/701210  S.NO=9876546V.F=9876546FLAGS=10100000000
7/703170  FLD7=9876546  FLAGS=10100000000
8/703420  FLD7=9876546  FLAGS=10100000000
8/703540  FLD7=9876546  FLAGS=10100000000
9/703690  FLD7=9876546  M=7 C=1 R=000 FLAGS=10100000000
9/703830  FLD7=9876546  M=2 C=7 R=193FLAGS=10100000000
9/703920  FLD7=9876546  INTR=187 RSLT=006
9/704010  FLD7=9876546  RSLT=006 FLAGS=10100000000
7/703320  FLD7=9876546  FLAGS=10100000000
2/701350  S.NO=9876546V.F=9876546FLAGS=10100000000
3/701500  QTY=      1V.F=0Q00001FLAGS=10100000000
8/703420  FLD7=0000001  FLAGS=10100000000
8/703540  FLD7=0000001  FLAGS=10100000000
```

UNUSED PART OF CARD

11 Appendix
Third test

```
MAN-ORDER     35   9876558      10000      --22220     D000200      5 690
                                                                    -----

1/400210 INPUT TRANSCODE 35
6/702390 DATE=05067EV.F=05067EFLAGS=0,000000000
6/702970 DATE=05067EVF F= 005067EFLAGS=1000001010
1/400280 ERROR FLAGS 1000001010

TRANSACTION CODE   STOCK NO.   QUANTITY   CUSTOMER   DESPCH NO.      DATE
        MAN-ORDER   35   9876558      10000     2222220    D000200      5 67E
                                                                    ------

1/400210 INPUT TRANSCODE 35
6/702390 DATE=050072V.F=050072FLAGS=0,000000000
6/702970 DATE=050072VF F= 0050072FLAGS=1000000001000
1/400280 ERROR FLAGS 1000001000

TRANSACTION CODE   STOCK NO.   QUANTITY   CUSTOMER   DESPCH NO.      DATE
        MAN-ORDER   35   9876558      10000     2222220    D000200      050072
                                                                    ------

1/400210 INPUT TRANSCODE 35
6/702390 DATE=051372V.F=051372FLAGS=0,000000000
6/702970 DATE=051372VF F= 0051372FLAGS=1000000001000
1/400280 ERROR FLAGS 1000001000
```

UNUSED PART OF CARD

UNUSED PART OF CARD

165

```
TRANSACTION CODE  STOCK NO.  QUANTITY  CUSTOMER  DESPCH NO.  DATE     UNUSED PART OF CARD
MAN-ORDER    35   9876558    10000     2222220   D000200     051372
                                                             ------

1/400210 INPUT TRANSCODE 35
6/702390 DATE=310472V.F=0310472FLAGS=00000000000
6/702670 DATE=310472V.F=0310472MAX-DAYS=30
6/702970 DATE=310472VF F= 0310472FLAGS=10000001000
1/400280 ERROR FLAGS 10000001000


TRANSACTION CODE  STOCK NO.  QUANTITY  CUSTOMER  DESPCH NO.  DATE     UNUSED PART OF CARD
MAN-ORDER    35   9876558    10000     2222220   D000200     310472
                                                             ------

1/400210 INPUT TRANSCODE 35
6/702390 DATE=000472V.F=0000472FLAGS=00000000000
6/702970 DATE=000472VF F= 0000472FLAGS=10000001000
1/400280 ERROR FLAGS 10000001000


TRANSACTION CODE  STOCK NO.  QUANTITY  CUSTOMER  DESPCH NO.  DATE     UNUSED PART OF CARD
MAN-ORDER    35   9876558    10000     2222220   D000200     000472
                                                             ------

1/400210 INPUT TRANSCODE 35
6/702390 DATE=290271V.F=0290271FLAGS=00000000000
6/702670 DATE=290271V.F=0290271MAX-DAYS=28
6/702970 DATE=290271VF F= 0290271FLAGS=00000000000
1/400280 ERROR FLAGS 00000000000
1/400210 INPUT TRANSCODE 35
6/702390 DATE=AB0272V.F=0AB0272FLAGS=00000000000
6/702970 DATE=AB0272VF F= 0AB0272FLAGS=10000001010
1/400280 ERROR FLAGS 10000001010


TRANSACTION CODE  STOCK NO.  QUANTITY  CUSTOMER  DESPCH NO.  DATE     UNUSED PART OF CARD
MAN-ORDER    35   9876558    10000     2222220   D000200     AB0272
                                                             ------

1/400210 INPUT TRANSCODE 00
1/400280 ERROR FLAGS 1011000101
```